ZERMATT
TRAVEL GUIDE
2024

Making Memories That Last a
Lifetime in Zermatt

CAROLINE ZAHN

Title: ZERMATT TRAVEL GUIDE 2024
Author: Caroline Zahn

Copyright © 2023 by Caroline Zahn

All right reserved. No part of this ebook may be reproduced, distributed, or transmitted in any form or by any means, including photocopying, recording, or other electronic or mechanical methods, without the prior written permission of the author, except in the case of brief quotations embodied in critical reviews and certain other non commercial uses permitted by copyright law. This book is a work of fiction,Names, characters, places and incidents are either products of the author's imagination or used fictitiously. Any resemblance to actual persons, living or dead ,event ,or locales is entirely coincidental

Cover design by: [Caroline Zahn]

Interior design and formatting by: [Caroline Zahn]
For inquiries regarding permission , please contact the author at: [carolinezahn@gmail.com]
First edition : [December 2023]
ISBN: [N/A]

ABOUT THE AUTHOR

Caroline Zahn is a gifted writer who has a love of discovery and the capacity to lead other adventurers on the most amazing adventures. With the help of his extensive guidebook, Caroline Zahn turns routine travels into amazing experiences. His work is evidence of his enduring wanderlust and his commitment to providing fellow travelers with priceless wisdom.

As an experienced tourist, Caroline Zahn is aware of the subtleties involved in seeing new locations and engaging with other cultures. His guides are painstakingly written to provide cultural subtleties. His real love for discovering lesser-known aspects of places is evident in every page of his work, which equips readers with the necessary knowledge to set off on unforgettable journeys.

Caroline Zahn's work is distinguished by its captivating language and painstaking attention to detail. He has a natural capacity to take readers to distant places, allowing them to see themselves in the colorful villages, quiet countryside, and busy marketplaces he so eloquently describes. His enlightening travel advice transcends the apparent and gives readers a thorough grasp of the destinations they are going to see.

Caroline Zahn travel guides are a priceless asset, regardless of your level of experience and desire for new insights. Through his efforts, tourists are not only able to arrange a smooth trip but also thoroughly immerse themselves in the beauty and authenticity of their surroundings.

With Caroline Zahn as your travel advisor, you can expect an adventure that will change and enrich you and leave a lasting impression on your heart and spirit.

ZERMATT TRAVEL GUIDE 2024

TABLE OF CONTENTS

CHAPTER 1: INTRODUCTION
- WELCOME TO ZERMATT
- BRIEF HISTORY OF ZERMATT
- GEOGRAPHY AND CLIMATE

CHAPTER 2: PLANNING YOUR TRIP
- BEST TIME TO VISIT
- DURATION OF STAY
- BUDGETING AND EXPENSES
- ESSENTIAL TRAVEL TIPS

CHAPTER 3: GETTING TO ZERMATT
- TRANSPORTATION OPTIONS
- ARRIVING BY AIR
- TRAIN AND CAR TRAVEL

CHAPTER 4: ACCOMMODATION
- HOTELS IN ZERMATT
- COZY BED AND BREAKFASTS
- VACATION RENTALS
- LUXURY RESORTS

CHAPTER 5: EXPLORING ZERMATT
- THE ICONIC MATTERHORN

- ZERMATT VILLAGE WALKTHROUGH
- TOP ATTRACTIONS AND LANDMARKS
- OFF THE BEATEN PATH DISCOVERIES

CHAPTER 6: OUTDOOR ADVENTURES
- HIKING TRAILS
- SKIING AND SNOWBOARDING
- MOUNTAIN BIKING
- PARAGLIDING AND ADVENTURE SPORTS

CHAPTER 7: CULINARY DELIGHTS
- TRADITIONAL SWISS CUISINE
- BEST RESTAURANTS IN ZERMATT
- COZY CAFÉS AND BAKERIES

CHAPTER 8: NIGHTLIFE AND ENTERTAINMENT
- BARS AND PUBS
- CULTURAL EVENTS AND FESTIVALS
- EVENING STROLLS AND VIEWS

CHAPTER 9: SHOPPING IN ZERMATT
- SOUVENIR SHOPS
- LOCAL ARTISANS AND CRAFTS
- HIGH-END BOUTIQUES

CHAPTER 10: WELLNESS AND RELAXATION
- SPA AND WELLNESS CENTERS
- YOGA AND MEDITATION
- HOT SPRINGS AND THERMAL BATHS

CHAPTER 11: DAY TRIPS FROM ZERMATT
- GORNERGRAT RAILWAY
- ZERMATT TO CERVINIA (ITALY)
- ZERMATT TO ZERMATT VALLEY

CHAPTER 12: PRACTICAL INFORMATION
- LANGUAGE AND CURRENCY
- EMERGENCY INFORMATION
- USEFUL CONTACTS

CHAPTER 13: SUSTAINABILITY IN ZERMATT

- ECO-FRIENDLY PRACTICES
- RESPONSIBLE TOURISM INITIATIVES

CHAPTER 14: CONCLUSION
- MEMORABLE EXPERIENCES
- PLANNING YOUR NEXT VISIT

CHAPTER 1: INTRODUCTION

WELCOME TO ZERMATT

Welcome to Zermatt, the beautiful Alpine paradise at the foot of the iconic Matterhorn! When you enter this charming Swiss village, the highest point of the Alps will greet you and you will be amazed by the beautiful panorama. Zermatt is more than a place; It is an experience that combines beauty, outdoor fun, and the charm of the mountains.

With its unique pyramid shape, the Matterhorn dominates the skyline and is your constant companion throughout your stay in Zermatt. This iconic mountain is one of the most famous mountains in the world, a symbol of Switzerland, and a source of inspiration for climbers and nature lovers.

The fact that Zermatt is a car-free city increases the city's special charm. Upon arrival, you'll notice the absence of traffic noise, replaced by the gentle sounds of horse-drawn carriages and the occasional chiming of cowbells. Stroll through the cobblestone streets, lined with charming chalets adorned with flower-filled balconies, and immerse yourself in the tranquil atmosphere of this alpine haven.

Adventure beckons in Zermatt, whether you're an avid skier, hiker, or simply a lover of the great outdoors. The region boasts an extensive network of hiking trails, catering to all skill levels. In winter, the slopes come alive with skiers and snowboarders carving their way through the fresh powder. The Gornergrat Railway provides a beautiful journey to take in the views of the surrounding landscape.

After a day of research, enjoy Zermatt's famous hospitality. There are many restaurants in the village serving delicious Swiss and international cuisine. After a day in the mountain air, you can warm up with a hearty meal such as a casserole or a cheese plate.

As the sun sets, Zermatt's charm begins to emerge. The village is bathed in golden light and the Matterhorn bursts into beautiful colors. Whether you choose to relax in a cabin in the cocoa mountains, drink hot cocoa in a charming cafe, or stroll under the stars, Zermatt promises a wonderful evening.

Welcome to Zermatt, where the splendor of nature meets the elegance of the Alps; invites you to explore, relax, and create memories in the heart of the Swiss Alps. Whether you're looking for adventure on the slopes, peace in the mountains, or an escape from the ordinary, Zermatt welcomes you with open arms.

BRIEF HISTORY OF ZERMATT

Zermatt's history is deep with the beautiful surrounding Alpine landscape and its story has been shaped by human efforts and natural forces. Here is a brief description of the historic route of the iconic Swiss village:

1. Early Settlement: The Zermatt Valley has evidence of human settlement dating back to prehistoric times. The first settlements were agricultural; communities were engaged in agriculture and animal husbandry in the harsh Alpine environment.

2. The rise of tourism: With the development of mountaineering in the 19th century, Zermatt began to turn into a tourism destination. British mountaineer Edward Whymper climbed the Matterhorn in 1865, sparking international interest in the area. This event marked the beginning of Zermatt's reputation as a major destination for climbers and adventurers.

3. Infrastructure Development: With the interest in the mountains, Zermatt has witnessed infrastructure developments to accommodate more visitors. Hotels, hostels, and transport facilities, including the Gornergrat Railway, were built to meet the needs of tourists.

4. The Golden Age of Mountaineering: Zermatt became the center of the "Golden Age of Mountaineering",

which took place in the 19th and early 20th centuries when climbers from all over the world could travel to the Alps to conquer their peaks. The village is the base of many expeditions and hikers have left an indelible mark on the region.

5. Tourism and car-free: In the 20th century, Zermatt's appeal was not limited to mountain climbing, but also included winter sports such as skiing. The village also has a car-free policy to maintain its attractiveness and protect the environment. Today, visitors can still enjoy the safety of horse-drawn carriages and electric taxis as they roam the streets.

6. Cultural Heritage: Zermatt's cultural heritage is reflected in the longevity of mountaineering in traditional chalets, Alpine architecture, and local culture. The Matterhorn Museum is located in the

center of the village and provides information on the history of Zermatt and the challenges faced by the first climbers.

7. Modern Zermatt: Today Zermatt has become a world-famous tourist destination that perfectly blends tradition and modernity. It continues to attract nature lovers, adventure seekers, and peace seekers.

The village is still a symbol of Swiss hospitality and Alpine beauty, with the Matterhorn's eternal presence in the beautiful corner of the Alps. Zermatt's history is a testament to the enduring appeal of the mountains and the indomitable spirit of those who discovered, lived, and loved this extraordinary Alpine village.

GEOGRAPHY AND CLIMATE

Geography:

Zermatt, in the southern Swiss canton of Valais, at the foot of the iconic Matterhorn. The village is part of the Pennine Alps and is surrounded by a stunning panorama of towering peaks such as Dent Blanche, Obergabelhorn, and of course the majestic Matterhorn. The Pennine Alps create a rugged and dramatic landscape filled with deep valleys, cliffs, and pristine glaciers.

The village of Zermatt is located at approximately 1,620 meters (5,315 feet) above sea level, making it the highest point. The surrounding mountain scenery provides a beautiful setting for the village, creating a perfect environment that attracts tourists from all over the world.

Climate:

Zermatt has a typical Alpine climate with different seasons and weather conditions affected by its altitude. Here is an overview of Zermatt's climate throughout the year:

1. Summer (June-August): Zermatt experiences mild daytime temperatures during the summer months, with maximum temperatures ranging from 15 to 25 degrees Celsius (59 to 77 degrees Fahrenheit). longer days provide ample time for outdoor activities such as hiking, cycling, and mountain climbing. Alpine meadows are full of beautiful flowers and create a colorful texture against the landscape.

2. Autumn (September-November): As the days get shorter, autumn brings cooler weather. As the deciduous trees change color, the landscape turns into a canvas of warm tones and the air takes on a pungent

scent heralding the arrival of autumn. A quiet time in Zermatt, perfect for those looking for more peace during the change of seasons.

3. Winter (December-February): Winter in Zermatt is when the village is covered in snow and the landscape turns into winter, it is spectacular. Average daytime temperatures range from -2 to 7 degrees Celsius (28 to 45 degrees Fahrenheit). The area is a paradise for winter sports enthusiasts, with world-class skiing and snowboarding opportunities in the surrounding area.

4. Spring (March-May): As winter turns to spring, Zermatt slowly recovers. The days are getting longer and temperatures are starting to rise. Spring is a good season for high-altitude snow sports enthusiasts because there is still snow in the mountains.

Alpine plants have begun to come to life and the valley floor is dotted with blooming flowers symbolizing the post-winter feeling of nature. Zermatt's geography and climate make it a year-round destination, offering visitors a variety of activities and experiences in every season. Whether covered in snow or covered in mountain flowers, Zermatt's natural beauty remains constant throughout the year.

CHAPTER 2: PLANNING YOUR TRIP

BEST TIME TO VISIT

The best time to visit Zermatt depends on your interests and the type of experience you are looking for; because this charming Alpine village offers something special in every season. Here are the points for different times of the year and for all times of the year:

1. Summer (June to August):
- Activities: Summer is great for outdoor enthusiasts. The road is wide and the ground is green. This is the perfect time to go mountain biking, paragliding and admire the scenery.

- Climate: Daytime temperatures are mild (15 to 25 degrees Celsius or 59 to 77 degrees Fahrenheit), making exploration easier. It can be chilly at night, so dress in layers.

2. Spring (September-November):
    - Activities: Spring offers a quieter experience with fewer guests. The changing colors of the leaves create a beautiful area for walking and a great opportunity for photography.
    - Weather: The temperature is starting to drop from cold to mild. It's a good time to enjoy the fresh mountain air.

3. Winter (December-February):
    - Activities: Winter is a paradise for ice and snow lovers. Zermatt has grown

into a beautiful snow resort offering world-class skiing, snowboarding, and other winter sports. The festive atmosphere during the festival also increases interest.
- Weather: Cool, daytime high temperature -2 to 7 degrees Celsius (28 to 45 degrees Fahrenheit). The village and surrounding peaks are covered with snow.

4. Spring (March-May):
- Event: Spring is a transitional time when winter and spring come together. Skiing is still possible at higher altitudes, and hiking trails open when the snow melts.
- Weather: Temperatures are starting to rise and spring is coming. It is a great opportunity for those who

want to experience the view of winter and spring.

Notes:
- Tourists: Zermatt tends to get crowded in summer and winter. If you prefer a quieter experience, consider visiting during the shoulder season, such as late spring or early fall.
- Events & Festivals: See local events. Zermatt hosts many events and festivals throughout the year, such as the Zermatt Unplugged Music Festival and the Gornergrat Zermatt Marathon.
- Matterhorn Visibility: If seeing the Matterhorn is important, remember that the mountain can be covered in clouds at any time of the year. Clear skies are more common in the morning, so consider

starting early to see the best views.

Ultimately, the best time to visit Zermatt depends on your interests and the type of experience you want. Whether you enjoy winter sports, blooming flowers, or autumn, Zermatt offers a unique and fascinating experience in every season.

DURATION OF STAY

The best place to stay in Zermatt depends on your interests, the activities you plan to do, and whether you want to relax in the tranquility of the Swiss Alps or experience the thrill of outdoor adventure. Here are some points to help you decide how long to stay in Zermatt:

1. Short term (2-3 days):   If you're short on time, short stays are also available, long enough for you to

enjoy the best of Zermatt. Focus on major attractions such as the Gornergrat Railway for panoramic views, visit the Matterhorn Museum to learn about local history, and travel through car-free towns through beautiful scenery. You can spend a day skiing or snowboarding in the winter, or check out some of the lower trails in the summer.

2. One-Week Retreat (5-7 days): A week in Zermatt allows you to explore more and gives you time to do more activities. You can make time for iconic hikes such as the Five Lakes Trail or the Gorner Gorge Trail, and explore neighboring areas such as the charming town of Zermatt. Winter visitors can enjoy long skiing or snowboarding, while summer visitors can enjoy more hiking and side activities.

3. Extended Stay (10+ days): For those looking for a truly unique experience, an extended stay allows you to step outside the usual tourist crowds. Dive deeper into more challenging hikes, explore trails less traveled, and take part in unique activities like climbing lessons or forest walks. Long-term stays also offer opportunities to experience local culture, eat fine cuisine, and participate in winter and summer sports depending on the season.

Notes:

- Seasonal changes: The time of year may affect the length of your stay. Winter enthusiasts will need more time to explore major ski areas, while summer visitors will be able to devote more time to hiking and outdoor activities.
- Event Calendar: See special events, holidays, or events

happening when you plan to stay. Many events are held in Zermatt throughout the year, and combining your visit with one of these can enhance your experience.
- Relax and Relax Adventure: Consider whether you want to relax, admire the scenery, and enjoy the peace, or are you looking for an adventure with lots of outdoor activities?

Ultimately, your stay in Zermatt depends on your interest and the experience you want to have in this charming Alpine village. Whether you're here for a short stay or a long adventure, Zermatt offers you a unique and unforgettable experience in the heart of the Swiss Alps.

BUDGETING AND EXPENSES

Zermatt is a luxury Alpine destination, but Switzerland in general is very expensive so it's important to plan your budget. Here are some tips for budgeting and managing your expenses while in Zermatt:

1. Accomodation: Accommodation options in Zermatt range from luxury hotels to comfortable chalets. Prices can vary greatly depending on the season and the type of service you choose. For a cheaper option, consider staying in a chalet or hotel. Booking in advance can help you get a better price.

2. Dinner: Dining in Zermatt can be a great experience, but restaurant prices may be higher than other places. Try to balance meals with cheaper options. Explore the local market or

market for snacks and consider dining at one of the attractions to enjoy your surroundings without paying for a restaurant.

3. Transportation: Since Zermatt is a village closed to vehicle traffic, transportation in the village is provided by electric taxis and horse carriages. These can be expensive, so budget accordingly. If you plan to explore nearby areas, consider purchasing a regional card or travel pass to get discounts on public transportation.

4. Sports: Outdoor activities such as skiing, snowboarding, and hiking may be subject to applicable equipment, carry-on, or travel fees. Research prices in advance and decide how you'll spend money on specific experiences that suit your interests.

5. Matterhorn Glacier Paradise: Matterhorn Glacier Paradise is accessible from the Gornergrat Railway and is a popular attraction. Check out ticket prices and decide if you can fit this wonderful experience into your budget.

6. Events and Festivals: Zermatt hosts many events and festivals throughout the year. Check the events on the calendar and include the associated costs in your budget if there is a special event you want to attend.

7. Souvenirs and Shopping: There are many souvenir and food shops in Zermatt. If you plan to bring home souvenirs or local items, set aside a shopping budget.

8. Currency: Swiss Franc (CHF) is used in Switzerland. Check current exchange rates and learn about the

best exchange rates. There are various ATMs in Zermatt for easy withdrawals.

9. Tipping: The Swiss have a habit of tipping, but this does not necessarily include service charges. Be prepared to tip approximately 10-15% of the restaurant or services.

10. Travel Insurance: Consider purchasing travel insurance that covers unexpected expenses such as medical emergencies or trip cancellations.

Tip:

- Off-Season Travel: Consider traveling off-season to save on accommodations and activities.
- Package Deals: Look for package deals that include accommodation,

transportation, and activities as these can save money.
- Local Transport Card: Explore the possibility of purchasing a local transport card that allows unlimited travel on local public transport.

By carefully planning and budgeting your trip to Zermatt, you can make the most of the Swiss Alps without breaking the bank. Adjust your budget based on personal preferences and priorities to create a memorable and financially manageable experience in this beautiful mountain village.

ESSENTIAL TRAVEL TIPS

Traveling to Zermatt, an idyllic Alpine village at the foot of the Matterhorn, requires some thought to get the most out of your experience. Our top travel tips to ensure a safe and enjoyable trip:

1. Pack properly: The weather in Zermatt is unpredictable, so wear outer layers to adapt to temperature changes. Please bring waterproof goggles, especially if you plan to explore the outdoors.

2. Shoes: Comfortable, waterproof shoes are a must, especially if you plan to hike or walk to many places. Make sure your shoes are suitable for urban and mountain environments.

3. Acclimatization to Altitude: Zermatt's high altitude may affect some people. Stay calm on the first day, stay hydrated, and consider taking medication if you're prone to heartburn.

4. Sun protection: The sun can be strong in the mountains. Bring sunscreen, sunglasses, and a hat to

protect yourself, especially when working outdoors.

5. Car-Free Village: Zermatt is a car-free village. Plan your arrival accordingly, and be prepared to use electric taxis, horse-drawn carriages, or your own two feet to navigate the charming streets.

6. Train Travel: The Swiss rail system is efficient and well-connected. If you're arriving by train, Zermatt is easily accessible. Consider purchasing a Swiss Travel Pass for seamless travel within the country.

7. Booking Accommodation: Zermatt offers a range of accommodation, but it can be in high demand, especially during peak seasons. Book your stay in advance and consider staying in a tent or tent for the ultimate experience.

8. Financial Decisions: Switzerland is known for its high cost of living. Plan your budget accordingly and cover meals, activities, and transportation expenses.

9. Language: German is the official language, but English is also widely spoken, especially in tourist areas. Learn basic German words for more information.

10. Local Cuisine: Try Swiss dishes like fondue and raclette. Although eating out can be expensive, experiencing local cuisine is part of travel.

11. Respect for local traditions: Switzerland is famous for its cleanliness and order. Contribute to your community's environmental efforts by respecting local traditions, including recycling and waste disposal procedures.

12. Safety first: Zermatt is a safe place, but accidents can happen, especially in the mountains. When participating in outdoor activities, please follow safety instructions and be aware of your surroundings.

13. Matterhorn View: The Matterhorn is sometimes covered with clouds. To get the best views, plan to visit in the morning when visibility is clearer.

14. Water Quality: Tap water in Switzerland is safe to drink. Carry a reusable water bottle to stay hydrated, especially when working outdoors.

15. High Season Plans: Zermatt can get busy during high season, so plan accordingly. For more fun, consider going in the off-season.

Keep these top travel tips in mind; You'll be prepared to make the most of Zermatt's natural beauty, outdoor adventures, and rich culture. Travel safely!

CHAPTER 3: GETTING TO ZERMATT

TRANSPORTATION OPTIONS

Zermatt is a car-free village with outstanding transport links in the beautiful Alps region. The main means of transportation in Zermatt are

1. Electric taxis: The streets of Zermatt are powered by electric taxis, which are the main means of transportation in the village. These taxis are environmentally friendly and help create a peaceful environment in a pedestrianized area.

2. Horse-drawn carriages: Another good way of transportation in Zermatt is horse-drawn carriages. These horse-drawn carriages offer a fun and beautiful way to explore the village, providing an amazing Alpine experience.

3. Hiking: Zermatt is a hiking village with good walking paths. Most attractions, shops, and restaurants are within walking distance, allowing visitors to easily explore the city. The car-free route is the highlight of the Zermatt experience.

4. Bicycles: Bicycles are a popular and environmentally friendly means of transport in Zermatt. The village has a dedicated bicycle path and many hotels provide free bicycles to their guests. Exploring Zermatt on two wheels offers flexibility and harmony with the natural environment.

5. Cable Cars and Cable Cars: Zermatt's mountain landscape is well served by a network of cable cars and cable cars. These services provide access to the surrounding area, which offers beautiful views of the Alps. For example, the Gornergrat Railway takes visitors to the top of the Gornergrat for panoramic views of the Matterhorn.

6. Mountain Railway: Zermatt has a well-established railway connecting the village to various mountain regions. Besides the Gornergrat Railway, the Sunnegga Cable Car and the Klein Matterhorn Cable Car (Matterhorn Glacier Paradise) are popular options for reaching higher altitudes.

7. Private Shuttle and Transfer Services: Some hotels and holiday villages offer private shuttle services to assist with transfer to the village.

These services may also include transportation to nearby attractions and airports.

8. Car Rental: Although Zermatt does not have a car, tourists can park in the nearby town of Täsch. From Täsch you can continue to Zermatt by train or taxi.

9. Electric Bus: Electric buses operate on special routes in the village, providing additional transportation opportunities to visitors. These buses connect the main places of Zermatt, making it easier for tourists to explore different places.

Transportation to visit Zermatt is part of the adventure, offering a unique and intimate experience in the beautiful Alps region. Whether you take an electric taxi through the village, enjoy a horse-drawn carriage ride, or take the train to the top of the mountain, transportation in Zermatt is designed to complement the beauty of the surroundings.

ARRIVING BY AIR

Although Zermatt does not have an airport, those arriving by plane usually land at one of Switzerland's major international airports and then drive to the village without a car. The two most convenient airports for transportation to Zermatt are Geneva Airport (GVA) and Zurich Airport (ZRH). Instructions for arriving and departing Zermatt by plane are as follows:

1. Landing at Geneva Airport (GVA) or Zurich Airport (ZRH): Geneva Airport is on the east side of Switzerland in autumn, and Zurich Airport is on the west. Switzerland. The country to the west of Switzerland. The country is located in the west of Switzerland.

Central region of the country. Both airports are well-connected and are major transit points for international travelers.

2. From Geneva Airport to Zermatt: You can take the train from Geneva Airport to Zermatt. The journey takes 3 to 4 hours and offers beautiful views of the Swiss countryside. Trains run regularly from the airport to Zermatt with transfers to cities such as Lausanne or Visp. Alternatively, you can arrange a transfer to the nearby Geneva train station or take a taxi and catch the direct train to Zermatt.

3. Zurich Airport to Zermatt: The train journey from Zurich Airport to Zermatt takes approximately 3 to 4 hours. Trains run regularly and you can change cars in cities such as Bern or Visp. This scenic route offers a glimpse of Switzerland's beautiful landscape. Another option is to take

the train to Zurich Central Station and then change to the direct train to Zermatt.

4. Transportation to Zermatt by train: Zermatt's train station is in the city center, so it is easy to reach. The railway is part of the experience with panoramic views of the Alps. If you come in your car, you can go to the last point, Taş city, by private vehicle. From Täsch you can take the bus to Zermatt. Visitors are encouraged to park in the car park at Tash.

5. Private Transfers: Private transfers can be arranged from the airport to Zermatt with various transportation options. This option provides convenience and flexibility to customize your trip to fit your schedule.

6. Transfer to helicopter: For a nicer and faster arrival, some travelers

prefer to go to Zermatt directly by helicopter. Helicopter services are available at both Geneva and Zurich airports.

Tips:

- Train tickets: To ensure availability and get the best prices, buy your train tickets in advance, online or at the airport train station.
- Luggage Transport: If you are traveling by train, consider the convenience of luggage. Some services allow you to check your luggage at the airport, which will be delivered directly to your hotel in Zermatt.
- Weather Warning: Please note that there may be weather-related delays during the winter months. Check the train schedule and weather

forecast, especially if traffic is fast.

Getting to Zermatt by plane is a beautiful experience and allows you to easily travel from the airport to the heart of the Swiss Alps. Whether you choose to take a scenic train tour or transfer, the journey itself will become an important part of your Zermatt experience.

TRAIN AND CAR TRAVEL

Zermatt Train Tour:

1. Scenic Rail Tour: Zermatt is famous for its good and beautiful connections. Take the train to Zermatt and enjoy the beautiful views of the Swiss Alps through beautiful mountains and charming villages.

2. Zermatt Train Station: Zermatt Train Station is located in the city

center. This car park is a major transportation hub where visitors can easily reach hotels, restaurants, and many attractions by electric taxi or horseback riding.

3. Access to nearby peaks: Zermatt railway provides transportation to the peaks and nearby areas. Famous examples include the Gornergrat Railway (which takes you to the top of the mountain for panoramic views) and the Sunnegga Funicular (which leads to Sunnegga Paradise for hiking and skiing).

4. Swiss Travel Pass: Consider purchasing the Swiss Travel Pass, which allows unlimited travel on trains and buses throughout Switzerland, including Zermatt. The route also includes some mountain railways and boats, providing a cost-effective and easy way to explore Switzerland.

5. Luggage Service: Some train services offer a luggage service that allows you to check your luggage at the airport or train station and deliver it directly to your hotel in Zermatt. This can be easily improved, especially if you plan to explore the village as soon as you arrive.

Driving to Zermatt:

1. Car-free village: Zermatt is a car-free village, which means that private cars are not allowed within the village boundaries. Visitors must park their vehicles in the nearby town of Tash, which is the last stop accessible by private vehicles.

2. Täsch Parking: There is a parking area in Täsch where visitors can easily catch the bus to Zermatt. The train journey from Täsch to Zermatt takes approximately 12 minutes.

3. Taxi and shuttle service: Zermatt has an electric taxi and shuttle service for guests in the village. These eco-friendly options create a peaceful environment and make traveling easier.

4.Parking Options: If you choose to drive to Tash, be sure to check for parking availability. The parking lots of many hotels in Taş also provide a convenient solution for visitors with cars.

5. Easy to explore the surroundings: Although Zermatt does not allow private cars, having a car makes it easier to explore the surroundings before arriving in Täsch. The drive itself is beautifully scenic and you can stop at the views along the way.

Information:

- Train tickets and reservations: Buy train tickets in advance and consider booking a nice walk, especially during the travel season.
- Car Rental: If you plan to rent a car, please be aware of parking restrictions in Zermatt. Choose somewhere in Rash with parking and easy access to buses.
- Airport Time: Check the train schedule and take into account the duration of your journey to optimize your time in Zermatt, especially if you have a private or sightseeing business.

Both train and car travel have similar advantages to reach Zermatt; Choosing between them depends on your preferences, time, and travel plans. Whether you choose the scenic railway or an easy drive, Zermatt awaits with its Alpine charm and stunning views.

CHAPTER 4: ACCOMMODATION

HOTELS IN ZERMATT

Surrounded by the majestic Swiss Alps and dominated by the iconic Matterhorn, Zermatt has many hotels to suit the different tastes and needs of its visitors. From luxury accommodations to cozy chalets, Zermatt offers many ways to have an unforgettable stay. Here is a summary of hotels in Zermatt:

1. Luxury Hotels: Zermatt is home to many of the world's best luxury hotels, all offering excellent service, spectacular views, and high-end products. These amenities often

include spa facilities, dining options, and personalized service. Some luxury hotels also have private wellness centers and private balconies with mountain views.

2. Boutique Hotels: Boutique hotels in Zermatt blend unique charm with personalized services. These establishments often have a distinctive character, reflecting the alpine surroundings and offering an intimate and cozy atmosphere. Boutique hotels may feature stylish décor, smaller room counts, and a focus on individualized guest experiences.

3. Mountain Lodges: For a more rustic and traditional experience, mountain lodges provide a cozy and authentic atmosphere. These accommodations often feature wooden interiors, alpine décor, and a warm ambiance. Mountain huts are ideal for those

looking for a feeling of home and connection with the natural environment.

4. Ski-In/Ski-Out Hotel: Zermatt is a famous winter sports resort and the ski-in/ski-out hotel appeals to ski and snowboard enthusiasts. These hotels have direct access to the ski area, making it easy for guests to head to the mountains for a day of fun. Ski-in/ski-out services often come with ski resorts, giving you the convenience of being close to the action.

5. Family-Friendly Hotels: Zermatt welcomes families and has many family-friendly hotels. These properties often have amenities for children, such as playgrounds, kids' meals, and family suites. Some family hotels also offer babysitting services, so parents can enjoy their stay while the kids play.

6. Budget and mid-range hotel options: Although Zermatt is best known for its luxury hotels, there are also budget and mid-range hotels available for travelers looking for more financial help. These accommodations offer comfortable rooms, and basic amenities and are a convenient base for exploring Zermatt without breaking the bank.

7. Wellness Hotels: Zermatt's wellness hotels focus on wellness, offering spa, fitness, and relaxation facilities. After a day of outdoor activities, guests can relax with massages, saunas, and other treatments. These hotels are often important for rejuvenation and relaxation.

8. Stylish and modern hotels: Some of Zermatt's hotels have a stylish and modern design. A beautiful and modern space can have stylish

interiors, technology, and stylish furniture. These hotels attract guests who enjoy the beautiful surroundings of the Alps region.

Tips for booking hotels in Zermatt:
- Spring: Zermatt can get busy in the high season, so book your accommodation in advance, especially if you plan to visit in the winter for skiing or summer hiking.
- Location: To make this easier, consider your hotel's location relative to local attractions, transportation, and your activities.
- Amenities: Check each hotel's amenities, such as spa facilities, dining rooms, and room amenities, to make sure they suit your preferences.
- Package Deals: Some hotels in Zermatt offer package deals that may include

accommodation, meals, and outdoor activities. Explore these options to save money.

Zermatt has a wide range of hotels, so visitors can find the best accommodation to suit their interests, whether they are looking for luxury, culture, or a combination of the two. With the beautiful Alps as a backdrop, hotels in Zermatt add to the charm and charm of this Swiss mountain village.

COZY BED AND BREAKFASTS

While Zermatt is best known for its luxury hotels and mountain resorts, the village also has many comfortable bed and breakfasts for socializing and staying at home. These charming hotels often offer a warm atmosphere along with personalized service to create a memorable stay for travelers looking to connect with their destination. Here is a rundown of the best Bed and Breakfast hotels in Zermatt:

1. Charming atmosphere: The Bed and Breakfast in Zermatt exudes a charming and cozy atmosphere. These places are usually small, allowing owners to offer guests personal preferences and create a better environment.

2. Authentic Alpine Decor: Many B&Bs in Zermatt feature authentic Alpine décor with wooden furniture, cozy fabrics, and local products. Interior design often reflects the mountain surroundings, enhancing the overall Alpine experience.

3. Breakfast at home: As the name suggests, the highlight of the B&B experience is breakfast. Guests can enjoy a homemade breakfast, often prepared using local ingredients and

Swiss dishes. The community breakfast area fosters a sense of community among guests.

4. Personal Service: B&Bs in Zermatt are renowned for their service. From offering local tips and recommendations to assisting with travel planning, hosts often go above and beyond to ensure their guests have an enjoyable and comfortable stay.

5. Quaint and Comfortable Rooms: Bed and Breakfast accommodations are generally smaller but have a better relationship and environment. Most of the rooms are individually designed with attention to detail in decoration and furnishings to create a warm atmosphere.

6. Local Knowledge: The hostel owners are mostly local people with deep knowledge of the region. They

can provide valuable insight into hidden gems, little-known hikes, and local activities, allowing guests to experience Zermatt beyond the typical tourist.

7. Affordable Price: Hostels in Zermatt are more affordable than big hotels. This makes them an attractive choice for budget-conscious consumers looking for an authentic and comfortable experience.

8. Central location: Most hostels in Zermatt are located in the city center, providing easy access to local shops, restaurants, and public transport. Thanks to its central location, guests can easily explore the pedestrianized streets on foot.

Tips for choosing Zermatt Bed and Breakfast:
- Reviews and Ratings: Check online and reviews to get an

idea of previous guests' experiences and nice bed and breakfast services.
- Location: Consider the B&B's proximity to the city center and most popular attractions to ensure it matches your search interests.
- Facilities: Although bed and breakfast facilities are known for their convenience, you can check whether they have the necessary amenities according to your needs, such as Wi-Fi, private bathroom, and heating.
- Book in advance: Due to the small size of the Zermatt B&B, availability may be limited, especially during the high season. It is recommended that you make a reservation in advance to guarantee your stay.

Choosing a good bed and breakfast in Zermatt allows you to get to know the village in a real and intimate way. Personal service, local charm, and a warm atmosphere create the warm and welcoming atmosphere that Zermatt is famous for.

VACATION RENTALS

Vacation rentals in Zermatt offer a unique and flexible accommodation option for visitors looking for a more independent and home-like experience. Whether you're traveling with family or friends or simply prefer the autonomy of a self-catered stay, vacation rentals provide a range of options to suit different needs and preferences. Here's an overview of vacation rentals in Zermatt:

1. Variety of Options: Zermatt offers a diverse range of vacation rentals, from charming chalets and

apartments to spacious homes. These accommodations cater to different group sizes and preferences, providing options for couples, families, or larger travel parties.

2. Self-Catering Facilities: One of the primary advantages of vacation rentals is the presence of self-catering facilities. Fully equipped kitchens allow guests to prepare their meals, providing flexibility in dining schedules and catering to specific dietary preferences.

3. Home-Like Comfort: Vacation rentals aim to provide a home-like environment, offering more space and privacy compared to traditional hotel rooms. Guests can enjoy separate living areas, bedrooms, and amenities that contribute to a comfortable and personalized stay.

4. Local Immersion: Staying in a vacation rental allows visitors to immerse themselves in the local culture of Zermatt. Many rentals are designed with alpine aesthetics, providing an authentic experience that complements the stunning natural surroundings.

5. Flexible Accommodation: vacation rentals come in a variety of sizes and configurations, allowing travelers to choose accommodations that meet their specific needs. Whether you want a beautiful apartment for a romantic getaway or a spacious apartment for a family holiday, Zermatt holiday rentals have many options for you.

6. Stunning Views: Many Zermatt holidays feature stunning views of the surrounding mountains, including the iconic Matterhorn. Enjoying these views from the comfort of your

accommodation can enhance the overall experience of your stay in the Swiss Alps.

7. Group Discounts: For large groups or families, vacation rentals can be an affordable option compared to booking multiple hotel rooms. The ability to share different locations and spread the cost across multiple passengers can result in significant savings.

8. Flexible Booking Options: Zermatt vacation rentals often offer flexible booking options, including short- and long-term rentals. This change allows guests to tailor their stay to their vacation or travel plans.

Tips for booking a vacation rental in Zermatt:
- Booking Platform: Use a popular vacation rental brand to find a variety of options.

Websites and apps like Airbnb, Booking.com, and Vrbo offer many options with user reviews and ratings.
- Amenities: Check out amenities like Wi-Fi, laundry and parking. Make sure the rental property has the right features to meet your specific needs.
- Location: Make sure the vacation rental fits your search interests by considering its location near downtown, transportation options, and nearby attractions.
- Contact the host: Contact the host before booking to clarify questions, confirm check-in details, and confirm your arrival.

Zermatt holidays offer flexible, self-catering accommodation allowing visitors to enjoy the beauty of the Swiss Alps with all the comforts of home. Whether you're looking for a romantic getaway, family, or group getaway, Zermatt Resorts offers many ways to make your stay in the beautiful Alpine village even more comfortable.

LUXURY RESORTS

Zermatt, nestled in the Swiss Alps with the iconic Matterhorn as its backdrop, is home to luxurious resorts that offer a combination of unparalleled comfort, stunning vistas, and world-class amenities. These luxury resorts cater to discerning travelers seeking an opulent Alpine experience. Here's an overview of what you can expect from luxury resorts in Zermatt:

1. Spectacular Locations: Luxury resorts in Zermatt are strategically

located to provide breathtaking views of the surrounding mountains, including the Matterhorn. The stunning Alpine scenery becomes an integral part of your stay, with many resorts featuring panoramic terraces and private balconies.

2. Sumptuous Accommodations: Accommodations in luxury resorts are designed to provide the utmost comfort and style. Elegant rooms and suites often feature Alpine-style décor, luxurious furnishings, and high-end amenities. Some hotels also have private cabins that provide a unique and comfortable experience.

3. World Class Dining: Dining at one of Zermatt's luxury resorts is a pleasure. The on-site gourmet restaurant offers the best of Swiss and international cuisine. Guests can enjoy delicious meals prepared by

talented chefs while enjoying the beautiful ambiance of the dining area.

4. Wellness and Spa Facilities: Wellness and spa facilities are a hallmark of luxury resorts in Zermatt. State-of-the-art spas, saunas, and fitness centers are designed to provide relaxation and rejuvenation. Many resorts also offer a range of wellness treatments, massages, and yoga classes.

5. Exclusive Lounges and Bars: Luxury resorts feature exclusive lounges and bars where guests can unwind in sophisticated surroundings. Enjoy handcrafted cocktails, fine wines, and premium spirits in an elegant atmosphere.

6. Concierge: Zermatt Luxury Resort's concierge provides services beyond expectations for guests. From arranging private tours to making

reservations at prestigious restaurants, the concierge is dedicated to ensuring your stay is perfect and unforgettable.

7. Adventure and Sports: Despite their beautiful surroundings, many parks offer outdoor activities. Whether mountain touring, skiing, or snowboarding, these resorts offer guests the opportunity to discover the natural beauty of Zermatt under expert guidance.

8. Entertainment and Conference Facilities: Luxury resorts in Zermatt often offer great theater and conference facilities. Suitable for social meetings, weddings, and special occasions, these venues offer beautiful views for unforgettable meetings.

9. Exclusive Amenities: Guests of the luxury hotel can benefit from

privileged facilities such as private transportation, personal concierge, and personalized services. These additional services help provide self-awareness and patience.

10. Culture and entertainment: Some luxury hotels organize cultural and entertainment programs to enrich their guests. This includes art, live performances, and special experiences that highlight local culture and traditions.

Tips for choosing a nice place in Zermatt:
- Reviews and Ratings: Reviews and ratings of previous guests to understand other people's experiences and the level of service at the property.
- Location: Consider the resort's location relative to Zermatt's attractions and activities. You can choose the

location that suits your interests, whether close to the village center or with direct access to the ski area.
- Wellness Services: Evaluate health and spa services to ensure they meet your expectations for relaxation and rejuvenation.
- Seasonal Considerations: Depending on the time of year, consider whether the resort offers seasonal activities such as skiing in the winter or hiking in the summer.
- Package Deals: Some luxury hotels may offer packages that include accommodation, meals, and activities. Explore value-added options during your stay.

Zermatt's luxury hotels offer the perfect combination of luxury and beauty, offering you an unforgettable experience in the heart of the Swiss Alps. Whether you're looking for a romantic getaway, a family celebration, or a beautiful destination, these resorts create a beautiful setting amidst the majestic Alps.

CHAPTER 5: EXPLORING ZERMATT

THE ICONIC MATTERHORN

Matterhorn is the symbol of the Swiss Alps and one of the most famous and majestic mountains in the world. The Matterhorn towers over the charming village of Zermatt and attracts visitors from all over the world with its unique and beautiful pyramid shape. Here's a close-up of Zermatt's landmark Matterhorn:

1. Distinctive Appearance: The Matterhorn is famous for its unique and instantly recognizable pyramidal peak. It has four faces following the cardinal directions, creating a unique and majestic silhouette against the alpine sky.

2. Height and location: The Matterhorn is 4,478 meters (14,692 feet) above sea level and crosses the border between Switzerland and Italy. Valais is part of the Pennine Alps and its peak marks the border between Switzerland and Italy.

3. First Ascent: The first ascent of the Matterhorn is an important chapter in the history of mountaineering. On July 14, 1865, British mountaineer Edward Whymper and his team completed the summit. However, an accident occurred during the descent, resulting in the death of four climbers.

4. Climbing and Mountaineering: The Matterhorn has become an iconic and challenging mountain for climbers. Climbing the Matterhorn is a difficult task, and most climbers train extensively before attempting the climb. The Hornley route chosen

by Whymper and his team remains the preferred and desired route to the summit.

5. Viewpoints: While climbing the Matterhorn requires skill and experience, visitors to Zermatt can enjoy the beauty of the mountain from a variety of viewpoints. The Gornergrat Railway and the Klein Matterhorn Cable Car (Matterhorn Glacier Paradise) are popular tourist attractions and offer beautiful views of the Matterhorn.

6. Inspiration in Art and Literature: Matterhorn has been a source of inspiration for many artists, writers, and photographers. Its majestic beauty is reflected in paintings, texts, and photographs, making it an enduring symbol of the Alps.

7. Skiing and Winter Sports: Zermatt, close to the Matterhorn, is a well-

known winter sports destination. Skiers and snowboarders can enjoy the scenery around the Matterhorn, and the city's parks offer beautiful scenery for alpine skiing.

9. Night Illumination: The Matterhorn is illuminated at night, creating a fascinating view. This tradition is called the Matterhorn Glacier Palace and includes carvings on the north side of the mountain. Lights celebrate many events and occasions and add a magical touch to an already beautiful space.

10. Nature Reserve: The Matterhorn and its surroundings are part of nature. Conservation efforts aim to preserve the unique flora and fauna that thrive in mountainous regions.

11. Symbol of Switzerland: Matterhorn is not only the symbol of the Swiss Alps but also of Switzerland.

His iconic image appears on Toblerone packaging, further cementing his status as a national icon.

Whether admired from afar or conquered by experienced climbers, the Matterhorn is a testament to the beauty and charm of the Swiss Alps. Its grandeur combined with the charming village of Zermatt at the foot of the mountain creates an unforgettable destination for those seeking harmony with nature and mountain adventure.

ZERMATT VILLAGE WALKTHROUGH

Walking through the car-free village of Zermatt is a wonderful experience combining the magic of the Alps, beautiful scenery, and a mix of old and modern. Here's a close-up of the charming village of Zermatt:

1. Arrival at Zermatt train station: Most visitors arrive in Zermatt by train, thanks to the village train parking in the city center. When you get off the train, you are immediately greeted with fresh mountain air and views of the Matterhorn towering in the distance.

2. Electric taxis and horse-drawn carriages: Since Zermatt is a car-free city, electric taxis, and horse-drawn carriages are available at the station to transport guests and their cargo depending on their place of residence. These environmentally friendly transportation methods contribute to the peaceful atmosphere of the village.

3. Bahnhofstrasse - Main Street: Main Street Bahnhofstrasse is the center of Zermatt. It is full of boutiques, cafes, and restaurants that

invite visitors to have fun. The street is lively but still has a relaxed and inviting atmosphere.

4. Traditional Swiss Architecture: Zermatt's architecture reflects the Swiss mountain style. The chalet features a flowered balcony and a pitched roof, adding to the beautiful surroundings. Many buildings are decorated with intricate carvings and Alpine elements.

5. Swiss boutiques and souvenir shops: Bahnhofstrasse is full of Swiss boutiques and souvenir shops. You can buy Swiss watches, chocolates, traditional Swiss clothes, and souvenirs here to commemorate your visit.

6. Cozy cafes and restaurants: Quaint cafes and restaurants on the main street invite guests to enjoy Swiss cuisine. Enjoy a glass of hot Swiss

chocolate, a piece of cake, or a fondue experience in the atmosphere.

7. Village Square - Kirchplatz: Kirchplatz Village Square, historical buildings, and St. Besides Zermatt's location, events, markets, and festivals are frequently held in the area.

8. St. Mauritius Church: St. Mauritius Church is an important place in the village. Its tower stands in front of a mountain, and the interior of the church is decorated with beautiful stained glass windows and wooden details.

9. Zermatt Museum: The Zermatt Museum offers information about the history, culture, and heritage of the region. This is a great stop for anyone who wants to learn more about the evolution of Zermatt.

10. Electric Bus: Electric buses provide easy transportation to tourists by passing through special routes within the village. These buses support Zermatt's pedestrian-friendly route.

11. Alpine gardens and green spaces: There are beautiful alpine gardens and green spaces in Zermatt. Take a walk in these areas and admire the beautiful flowers, beautiful views, and serenity around you.

12. Observation Deck: Many observation decks in Zermatt offer beautiful views of the village and the Matterhorn. Popular tourist attractions such as Gornergrat and Sunnegga Paradise, are accessible by mountain railways and cable cars.

13. Matterhorn Museum: The Matterhorn Museum is dedicated to the history and culture of Zermatt and

the Alps. Located near the village square, it tells the fascinating story of the first ascent of the Matterhorn and the transformation of the village.

14. Hiking and nature: Zermatt is the gateway to many hiking and nature trails. Whether you're looking for a short hike or a more challenging hike, these hikes allow you to immerse yourself in beautiful mountain views.

15. Night Environment: When night comes, the town will spend time in a magical place with the sparkle of street lights and the ambiance of the mountains. Enjoy peaceful evenings on well-lit streets and relax in the peace of the Alps.

A walk through the village of Zermatt is a sensory journey filled with fresh mountain air, the sounds of cowbells, and beautiful pictures of huts with the Matterhorn in the background. Whether exploring great trails or wandering through the tranquil countryside, Zermatt offers the ultimate Alpine experience around every corner.

TOP ATTRACTIONS AND LANDMARKS

Nestled beneath the iconic Matterhorn in the Swiss Alps, Zermatt is a haven for outdoor enthusiasts and mountain adventure seekers. Not only is the village the gateway to exciting mountain adventures, but it also has a variety of attractions and landmarks that attract visitors. Here are some of the best views and areas in Zermatt:

1. Matterhorn: The Matterhorn is undoubtedly an iconic landmark that stands majestically as the symbol of Zermatt. Its pyramid-shaped peak can be seen from every point of the village and adds beauty to many events.

2. Gornergrat Railway: The Gornergrat Railway is a historic cog train that takes visitors to the top of Gornergrat Mountain. The journey offers panoramic views of the Matterhorn and surrounding peaks, making it one of the most scenic train rides in the world.

3. Klein Matterhorn (Matterhorn Glacier Paradise): The Klein Matterhorn, also known as the Matterhorn Glacier Paradise, is the highest cable car station in Europe. It provides access to stunning viewpoints, an ice palace, and the opportunity to stand at the foot of the Matterhorn.

4. Hiking Trails: Zermatt is a paradise for hikers, offering a network of well-marked trails suitable for various skill levels. Popular hikes include the Five Lakes Walk, the

Hörnli Hut trail, and the scenic path to the Hike to Schwarzsee.

5. Hörnli Hut: Hörnli Hut is a mountain hut located on the Hörnli Ridge of the Matterhorn. It is a famous base for climbers trying to climb the Matterhorn and has beautiful views of the mountains.

6. Zermatt Glacier Palace: The Glacier Palace on the Klein Matterhorn is an ice cave with tunnels and chambers that reveal the beautiful world beneath the glacier. Visitors can explore ice sculptures and crevices in the unique underground area.

7. Sunnegga Paradise: Accessible by Cable Car, Sunnegga Paradise is a sunny terrace with stunning views of the Matterhorn. It is a popular starting point for hiking and has a family park.

8. Gorner Gorge: Gorner Gorge is a wonder outside Zermatt. Tree walks take visitors through the forest to see waterfalls, rock formations, and the power of nature up close.

9. Zermatt Village Walk: Walk through the car-free village of Zermatt and experience its charm, traditional chalets, and beautiful atmosphere. On the streets of the village, you will come across grocery stores, cute cafes, and places such as the Saint-Mauritius Church.

10. Matterhorn Museum: The Matterhorn Museum in the heart of the village offers you a beautiful journey through Zermatt's history, mountain stories, and the heritage of the region. It gives you a view of the first ascent of the Matterhorn in 1865.

11. Church of St. Mauritius: St. Paul with its unique tower. Mauritius

village square is an important place. The interior of the church has beautiful stained glass windows and wooden elements, making it a quiet place to meditate.

12. Theodul Pass: Theodul Pass is a mountain pass connecting Zermatt with the Italian resort town of Cervinia. Visitors can reach the pass by cable car and enjoy panoramic views of the Matterhorn and surrounding peaks.

13. Zermatt Resort Area: Zermatt offers a range of luxury resorts, hotels, and accommodations surrounded by stunning alpine landscapes. Many of these establishments provide spa facilities, gourmet dining, and exclusive amenities.

14. Heli-Skiing and Heli-Sightseeing: For those seeking an adrenaline rush,

heli-skiing and heli-sightseeing tours offer an extraordinary perspective of the Matterhorn and the vast alpine terrain.

15. Alpine Gardens and Parks: Explore the alpine gardens and parks within Zermatt, such as the Hinterdorfstrasse Garden. These green areas provide a peaceful environment where you can enjoy the beauty of your surroundings.

Zermatt's sights and landmarks are the perfect combination of great views, rich culture, and entertainment. Whether admiring the Matterhorn, going on a hiking adventure, or exploring the cultural heritage of the village, Zermatt offers an unforgettable experience in the beautiful Swiss Alps.

OFF THE BEATEN PATH DISCOVERIES

bbbWhile Zermatt is best known for its iconic landmarks and attractions, there are also hidden gems and hidden gems that offer travelers a more curious and unique experience. Get off the beaten path and discover Zermatt's lesser-known wonders:

1. Lake Stellisee: The Five Lakes Walk is a popular route, while Lake Stellisee is a quieter option. Offering beautiful views of the Matterhorn, the pristine mountain lake offers a peaceful and beautiful retreat for those seeking solitude.

2. Walk to Fluhalp: Escape the crowds by walking to Fluhalp, a charming mountain hut in the Alps region. The road offers panoramic views of the surrounding peaks, and

Fluhalp itself is a peaceful haven away from the hustle and bustle.

3. Unterrothorn Peak: Consider hiking to Unterrothorn Peak for a unique view of the Matterhorn. This beautiful place offers a rare view of the iconic peak and surrounding mountain scenery.

4. Edelweiss and Zermatt Safari: Discover the Edelweiss and Zermatt Safari near Furi. This hidden gem is home to Alpine wildlife, and visitors can see mountain goats, marmots, and other animals in their natural habitat.

5. Hike to August Nordhorn: Head to a quiet place in the Alps with the Hike to August Nordhorn. This small road offers beautiful views of the Matterhorn and the surrounding mountains.

6. Trift Hut: Trift Hut is a mountain hut. It has a rustic and authentic mountain experience, surrounded by grass and panoramic views. A trip to Thrift is less crowded than some popular tourist attractions.

7. Schwarzsee: While many tourists head to Gornergrat, Schwarzsee is less known for its wonderful views of the Matterhorn. A trip to Lake Schwarzsee will allow you to enjoy the mountain views in a quiet place.

8. Find Alpine Flowers: Explore the alpine meadows around Zermatt and discover the many colorful alpine flowers. These beautiful flower posts add charm to the mountain landscape.

9. Findeln Historic Walser House: Discover the historic Walser House in Findeln, a charming little village above Zermatt. These wooden houses present the heritage of the Walzer

people, an Alpine community with a rich history.

10. Hike to Hörnli Hut (no meeting point): Although the challenge of the Matterhorn is difficult, the hike to Hörnli Hut is worth doing without difficulty. The hut itself offers beautiful views and the opportunity to witness the climbers' efforts.

11. Hidden Cafes and Restaurants: Get off the main road and discover hidden cafes and restaurants in the quiet part of Zermatt. These places often have more unique experiences and opportunities to sample local desserts.

12. Zmutt Village: Discover the charming village of Zmutt, located above Zermatt. This small village has no typical Swiss chalets and is a peaceful retreat away from the busy areas of Zermatt.

13. Winkelmatten Church: Visit the interesting church in the Winkelmatten area. This beautiful church is a hidden gem with a peaceful atmosphere and provides a place for quiet contemplation.

14. Lakeside Reflections: Find small lakes and ponds around Zermatt and enjoy tranquil views of the surrounding mountains. These peaceful places offer tranquility and opportunities to connect with nature.

15. Discover Hinterdorfstrasse: Walk along Hinterdorfstrasse, a quiet street in Zermatt with narrow streets and chalets. This place offers a glimpse into the history of the village and a better experience of mountain life.

Explore the area outside Zermatt; You will discover a world of wonders, tranquility, and unique views of the beautiful Swiss Alps. Whether you prefer to explore lesser-known paths, discover secret spots, or explore quieter parts of the village, there are many hidden treasures in Zermatt for those willing to search.

CHAPTER 6: OUTDOOR ADVENTURES

HIKING TRAILS

Surrounded by the stunning Swiss Alps and dominated by the iconic Matterhorn, Zermatt is a hiker's paradise. The area has a good network of hiking trails suitable for all skill levels, allowing you to immerse yourself in the beautiful mountain scenery. Here are some of Zermatt's famous trails:

1. Five Lakes Trail (5-Seenweg): This beautiful trail takes hikers around Gornergrat admiring the Matterhorn. This is an easy route suitable for all types of walkers and can be completed in a few hours.

2. Gornergrat Panorama Trail: For a longer hike, the Gornergrat Panorama Trail offers beautiful views of the Matterhorn and surrounding peaks. This route will take you from Gornergrat train station to Riffelberg, passing through many mountain regions.

3. Hiking to Hörnli Hut: Climbing the Matterhorn is a major mountain challenge, but hiking to Hörnli Hut is a great reward. The hut serves as a base camp for climbers attempting to summit the Matterhorn, and the trail offers spectacular views of the iconic mountain.

4. Schwarzsee to Hörnli Hut: This challenging trail runs from Schwarzsee to Hörnli Hut and passes through rocky terrain, offering beautiful views of the Matterhorn. This is a more desirable experience for

experienced hikers looking for adventure climbing.

5. Fluhalp to Zermatt: Travel from Fluhalp to Zermatt and avoid the crowds. The path takes you through alpine meadows with stunning views of the Matterhorn and offers a quiet and pleasant walk to the village.

6. Hiking to Lake Stellisee: Lake Stellisee is a hidden gem that can be reached by hiking from Blauherd or Sunnegga. This path offers a beautiful view of the Matterhorn in the clear mountain waters, making it beautiful and peaceful.

7. Europaweg: The Europaweg Trail is a long-distance hiking trail connecting Grechen and Zermatt. This is a challenging hike across continuous bridges and mountain terrain, offering panoramic views of the Matterhorn along the way.

8. Hike to Trift: Hike to Trift takes you to a mountain hut surrounded by meadows and beautiful views of the Matterhorn. This is a great trail that takes hikers through a quiet mountain region.

9. Hike to Riffelsee: Riffelsee is a small lake near Gornergrat. A trip to Lake Riffelsee offers a beautiful view of the Matterhorn reflected in the clear water. It is a short route suitable for half-day tours.

10. Gornerschlucht (Gorner Gorge) Route: Explore Gornerschlucht along the route passing wooden walkways and bridges to get closer to the waterfalls and unique rocks. This is a fun and family trip.

11. Sunnegga to Fluhalp hike: Starting from Sunnegga, this trail takes you to the Fluhalp mountain

hut. Walk; It has a variety of landscapes, including forests, alpine meadows, and spectacular views of the surrounding peaks.

12. Moiry Hut Road: For more fun, consider Moiry Hut Road. It leads to a mountain hut with panoramic views of the Matterhorn and the surrounding mountains. The route includes mountainous pastures and rocky lands.

13. Hike to Höhbalmen: This trail leads to the summit of Höhbalmen, which offers beautiful views of the Matterhorn. Alpine vegetation and panoramic views make this place ideal for nature lovers.

14. Planet Trail: Planet Trail is a work that represents the solar system with scaled-down planet models along the way. This is an informative,

family-friendly walk suitable for people of all ages.

15. Trek to Gorna Glacier: Trek to Gorna Glacier for a unique experience. This route will get you up close and personal with the glacier landscape and give you a glimpse of the beautiful ice and mountain scenery.

Always check the road conditions, the weather, and your own body before starting a walk in Zermatt. Whether you're looking for a stroll or a challenging mountain adventure, Zermatt's hiking trails offer a variety of experiences, all showcasing the stunning beauty of the Swiss Alps.

SKIING AND SNOWBOARDING

Zermatt is a world-renowned destination for skiing and snowboarding, attracting winter sports enthusiasts from around the globe with its extensive ski areas, diverse terrain, and stunning alpine scenery. Whether you're a seasoned pro or a first-time skier, Zermatt offers a winter wonderland of options for both skiing and snowboarding:

1. Matterhorn Glacier Paradise: The Matterhorn Glacier Paradise is one of the highest ski areas in Europe, and it offers year-round skiing and snowboarding. With a network of lifts and cable cars, you can ascend to breathtaking altitudes and enjoy the thrill of skiing against the backdrop of the iconic Matterhorn.

2. Ski Areas: Zermatt is part of the Matterhorn Glacier ski paradise, which includes interconnected ski areas in Switzerland and Italy. The Zermatt-Cervinia-Valtournenche ski domain provides access to a vast network of pistes and trails catering

to skiers and snowboarders of all levels.

3. Gornergrat Ski Area: The Gornergrat is not only a spectacular viewpoint, but it also offers a ski area with well-groomed slopes. From here, skiers and snowboarders can enjoy panoramic views of the surrounding peaks while navigating a variety of trails.

4. Skiing in the Sunnegga Paradise: Sunnegga is a popular skiing and snowboarding area accessible by funicular from Zermatt. The sunny slopes here cater to a range of skill levels, making it an ideal spot for families and beginners.

5. Zermatt Black Runs: For advanced skiers seeking a challenge, Zermatt has several black runs, including the famous "National" and "Klein Matterhorn" descents. These runs

offer steep slopes and demanding terrain, providing an adrenaline-filled experience.

6. Terrain Parks: Zermatt features terrain parks for snowboarders and freestyle skiers. These parks include features such as jumps, rails, and halfpipes, providing opportunities for riders to showcase their skills and enjoy a playful experience on the slopes.

7. Heli Skiing: For those seeking an off-piste adventure, heliskiing is available in the Zermatt area. Helicopters transport skiers and snowboarders to remote and untouched slopes, offering a thrilling and exclusive alpine experience.

8. Ski Schools and Lessons: Zermatt has reputable ski schools that cater to all levels, from beginners to advanced skiers and snowboarders. Private

lessons and group classes are available, allowing individuals to hone their skills or learn the basics in a supportive environment.

9. Après-Ski Scene: After a day on the slopes, Zermatt offers a vibrant après-ski scene. Enjoy cozy mountain huts, trendy bars, and lively restaurants where you can unwind, socialize, and celebrate a day of skiing or snowboarding.

10. Cross-Country Skiing: Zermatt provides opportunities for cross-country skiing on groomed trails. Peace and fresh mountain air make cross-country skiing a good choice for those who enjoy different sports.

11. Winter Ski Area: If you want to take a break from skiing or snowboarding, Zermatt offers winter trails that show off the beauty of the snow-covered Alps. The track is

suitable for all levels and has a variety of terrain.

12. Skiing at Gravity Park: Zermatt's Gravity Park is a special area for snowboard enthusiasts and has many areas such as jumps, ramps, and halfpipes. This is a popular place for freestyle skiers to hone their skills and enjoy the experience.

13. Ski and Snowboard Rental Shops: There are many shops in Zermatt where visitors can find good ski and snowboard equipment. Whether you're a beginner or an expert, these stores have a variety of products to suit your interests and skill level.

14. Night Skiing: Some ski resorts in Zermatt offer night skiing, allowing visitors to experience the excitement of skiing under the stars. The illuminated slopes create a magical

atmosphere, making your evening in the mountains unforgettable.

15. Summer Events and Competitions: Zermatt offers a variety of winter events and competitions, including ski competitions, freestyle competitions, and snowboard competitions. These events showcase the athletes' skills and increase the excitement of winter sports in Zermatt.

It is important to check the weather forecast, hiking maps, and safety tips before skiing. Whether you're blasting the flats, blasting the tough black tracks, or honing your skills in the park, Zermatt offers plenty of winter experiences to enjoy on the beautiful mountain slopes.

MOUNTAIN BIKING

Known for its majestic mountains and beautiful landscapes, Zermatt is not only a paradise for winter sports enthusiasts; It is also an exciting experience for those who love cycling in the summer months. With its beautiful trails, challenging descents, and beautiful mountain views, Zermatt has become a sought-after destination for mountain bikers. Here's a view of mountain biking in Zermatt:

1. Gornergrat Trail: The Gornergrat area offers a variety of mountain biking trails suitable for different skill levels. Riders can climb the trail using the Gornergrat Cable Car or an electric bike to enjoy views of the Matterhorn and the surrounding area.

2. Sunnegga Paradise Trails: Sunnegga Paradise is not only suitable for skiing in the winter months; In the summer it turns into mountain biking. Sunnegga's journey from the

forest path to the open offers a different journey.

3. Zermatt Bicycle Park: Zermatt Bicycle Park is designed for people who love cycling and cycling. The bike park features a variety of trails with jumps, berms, and slopes that provide an adrenaline-filled experience with the Matterhorn in the background.

4. Gornergrat to Riffelberg descent: For a great thrill, passengers can take the Gornergrat Bahn to the top of the mountain and then start descending. They can explore the slopes and go to Riffelberg. The trail has both technical and smooth downhill sections and spectacular mountain views.

5. Hörnli Road: The Hörnli Road takes cyclists from Hörnli Hut, known as the base camp of Matterhorn climbers, to Zermatt. This challenging route combines

technical techniques with mountain views, giving experienced riders a sense of accomplishment.

6. Schwarzsee descent: Schwarzsee is located near the Hörnli Hut and offers a competitive descent for cyclists. Combining rocky sections with steep descents, this route offers an adventurous journey with panoramic views of the Matterhorn.

7. Rothorn Trails: There are many trails in the   Rothorn area to suit all skill levels. Passengers can ascend using the Rothorn Bahn and descend through meadows and forests, as well as enjoy beautiful views of the surrounding mountains.

8. Gornerschlucht Road: The Gornerschlucht Road takes cyclists through the Gorner Gorge, offering a unique journey among wooden paths and bridges. This trip includes a drive

with beautiful canyon and waterfall views.

9. Cycling and Walking Routes: Zermatt offers cycling and walking routes that allow riders to combine mountain biking with mountain walks. These routes create an outdoor experience by offering the convenience of exploring on two wheels and foot.

10. Zermatt Electric Bikes: Electric mountain bikes (e-bikes) are very popular in Zermatt and allow riders to explore the mountains with less effort. E-bikes allow more enthusiasts to enjoy the beautiful scenery around Zermatt.

11. Guided Mountain Bike Tours: For beginner hikers or those looking for a guided tour, many companies are offering guided mountain bike tours in Zermatt. Local guides provide in-

depth knowledge of the area to ensure a safe and enjoyable walk.

12. Alpine Huts and Shelters: Some of the Zermatt mountain bike trails lead to mountain huts and shelters. These huts provide travelers with a beautiful place to relax, enjoy local cuisine, and breathe in the mountain air.

13. Bike Shop and Rental: has a bike shop and rental service in Zermatt that allows visitors to check out quality bikes, safety, and equipment. Whether you bring your bike or rent one in Zermatt, you'll find everything you need for your mountain biking adventure.

14. Mountain Bike Events: Zermatt hosts many mountain bike events and races throughout the summer. These events attract cyclists from all over the world and contribute to the region's mountain biking community.

15. Alpine landscapes and wildlife: A special feature of mountain biking in Zermatt is the opportunity to admire Alpine landscapes and wildlife. Riders will encounter prairie dogs, mountain flowers, and beautiful views as they make their way through the course.

Mountain bikers should check the trail, and weather conditions and comply with local regulations before hitting the trail. Whether you are looking for challenging mountain trails, scenic trails, or both, Zermatt offers an unforgettable cycling experience amid the unique beauty of the Swiss Alps.

PARAGLIDING AND ADVENTURE SPORTS

Located in the heart of the Swiss Alps, against the backdrop of the iconic Matterhorn, Zermatt is an adventure paradise year after year, not only for winter sports enthusiasts but also for adventure seekers. Paragliding and other adventure sports in Zermatt offer unique views of the beautiful mountain landscape. Here's a look at the world of paragliding and other fun activities in Zermatt:

1. Paragliding: Experience paragliding in Zermatt and soar like an eagle over the magnificent Swiss Alps. Experienced paragliding instructors offer competitive flights, allowing participants to experience the excitement of flight accompanied by views of the Matterhorn, mountain meadows, and glaciers.

2. Helicopter Tours: For a spectacular aerial adventure, helicopter tours from Zermatt offer bird's-eye views of the Matterhorn and surrounding peaks. Helicopter tours offer a unique

and stunning perspective of the mountain landscape.

3. Skydiving: Have the best skydiving experience in Zermatt. Jump from a plane high above the Swiss Alps and enjoy an unparalleled sense of freedom and excitement before landing in the mountain landscape below.

4. Via Ferrata: Zermatt has ferrata routes that allow adventurers to cross rock faces and cliffs using fixed cables, ladders, and bridges. The Gorner Gorge via Ferrata is a popular choice, offering spectacular climbing and views.

5. Canyoning: Embark on a canyoning adventure in the rugged terrain around Zermatt. Walk through narrow canyons and slide down natural rocks into clear mountain waters. Canyoning trips offer a

combination of discovery and excitement.

6. Rock Climbing: Zermatt is surrounded by beautiful peaks, making it a paradise for rock climbers. Whether you're a beginner or an experienced climber, there are routes and climbs for all skill levels that will provide you with challenges and benefits.

7. Mountain bike: Zermatt's extensive network of mountain bike routes appeals to riders looking for fun adventures. Downhill, hiking, and freeride options make Zermatt the perfect destination for cycling enthusiasts.

8. Bungy Jumping: For a leap of faith, consider bungee jumping in the Zermatt area. Jump from the high platform and feel the adrenaline rush as you plummet to the ground before

the jump rope brings you to a terrifying halt.

9. Alpine Coaster: Zermatt Forest Amusement Park includes the Alpine Coaster, an amusement ride through the forest. This gravity-based adventure combines speed and excitement against beautiful mountains.

10. Zipline Adventure: The Zipline experience in Zermatt allows participants to glide across the terrain, enjoying the wind and panoramic views. This zipline adventure offers an exciting way to experience the mountain scenery.

11. Summer Ski and Snowboard: Although Zermatt is best known for its winter sports, the summer months offer a unique opportunity to ski and snowboard on ice. The Matterhorn glacier paradise provides a high-

altitude playground for sports enthusiasts even in the warm season.

12. Electric Bike Adventure: Explore the mountain terrains with an electric mountain bike (e-bike). Zermatt's electric bike adventure tours offer an easy way to hit the road and discover the beauty of the Swiss Alps.

13. Adventure races and competitions: Zermatt hosts many adventure races and competitions throughout the year, attracting participants from all over the world. These activities often include mountain biking, hiking, and other recreational activities.

14. Nordic Walking Trail: If you're looking for a less strenuous but equally scenic adventure, discover Zermatt's Nordic Walking Trail. The road passes through meadows and forests, providing a peaceful way to experience the mountain scenery.

15. Adventure Park: The Adventure Park in and around Zermatt features high ropes courses, zip lines, and challenging obstacles. These parks offer family fun experiences suitable for many participants.

Always pay attention to safety and follow the instructions of experienced instructors before participating in any adventure sports in Zermatt. Whether you choose to soar through the sky with a paraglider, overcome rock walls with Ferrata, or experience the excitement of parachute jumping, Zermatt promises many heart-pounding adventures by challenging the unique beauty of the Swiss Alps.

CHAPTER 7: CULINARY DELIGHTS

TRADITIONAL SWISS CUISINE

Located in the heart of the Swiss Alps, Zermatt not only attracts visitors with its magnificent views but also offers a great culinary experience. Zermatt's traditional Swiss cuisine reflects the rich flavors of the region, combining local ingredients with Alpine influences. You can taste Swiss cuisine in Zermatt:

1. Fondue: When it comes to Swiss cuisine, there is no need to mention fondue. Like many parts of Switzerland, Zermatt is famous for fondue, a local dish in which a pot of cheese is served with bread cubes. The classic "moitié-moitié" fondue

combines two cheeses, usually Gruyère and Vashlin.

2. Rösti: Rösti is a Swiss potato dish that is a healthy side dish to many dishes. Fry grated potatoes until golden and crispy for a delicious meal. In Zermatt, you can find varieties that add ingredients such as cheese or bacon.

3. älplermagronen: älplermagronen, also known as Swiss Alps spaghetti; is a snack consisting of pasta, potatoes, cheese, and onions. Most of the ingredients are layered and baked to make a hearty and delicious casserole.

4. Cheese Plate: Cheese plates are a staple of Swiss cuisine, given the country's reputation for quality cheese. Zermatt has a variety of local cheeses such as Emmentaler, Gruyère, and Raclette. Enjoy this cheese with fresh bread, nuts, and fruit.

5. Zürcher Geschnetzeltes: Zürcher Geschnetzeltes is a Swiss dish you can find in Zermatt, although it is not specific to the Alpine region. It is made with thinly sliced beef cooked in a creamy mushroom and white wine sauce and served over noodles or rice.

6. Raclette: Raclette is another favorite Swiss cheese dish, especially popular in the Alps. Heat the raclette wheel and brush the pieces over the potatoes, pickles, and marinated meats. It is a good and healthy relationship.

7. Saffron Risotto: Zermatt's proximity to Italy has influenced its cuisine and Saffron Risotto is a dish that perfectly blends Swiss and Italian flavors. The addition of saffron gives risotto a unique taste and vibrant color.

8. Herbed Lamb Dishes: Alpine herbs and spices play an important role in flavoring Zermatt lamb dishes. Local herbs such as thyme, rosemary, and juniper are often used to enhance the flavor of lamb, resulting in a rich and delicious dish.

9. Swiss Chocolate: Although Swiss chocolate is not a food product, it is an important part of the Zermatt gastronomic experience. Enjoy fine Swiss chocolate, available in many flavors and types, from bars to pralines.

10. Bircher Muesli: Bircher Muesli is a popular Swiss breakfast dish that is a healthy and delicious combination of oatmeal, fresh fruit, nuts, and yogurt. Enjoyed all year round, this drink is a fresh and energetic way to start the day.

11. Zermatt Lamb: Zermatt is famous for its excellent lamb, mostly from local Alpine pastures. Zermatt's roast lamb dish showcases the quality and taste of meat produced in the region.

12. Apple Pie: Complete your meal with a classic Swiss dessert like apple pie. These cookies are filled with apples, raisins, and cinnamon and are usually served with a dollop of whipped cream.

13. Mountain Honey: Zermatt mountains are home to many plant species, resulting in a unique and sweet mountain honey. Drizzle local honey on bread, cheese, or dessert for a taste of the region.

14. Hearty soups: Alpine winters call for warm soups, and Zermatt dishes such as barley soup, minestrone, and minestrone are perfect for refueling after a day of poisoning outside.

15. Swiss Wine: Switzerland is famous for its fine wines and Zermatt offers the opportunity to try many local varieties. Pair Swiss wine with your meal to complement the flavor of Swiss food.

Whether you're chowing down on gooey cheese fondue, indulging in a comforting bowl of latke, or savoring local cheese delicacies, Zermatt's traditional Swiss cuisine offers something just as fascinating as mixed dishes in a mountainous region around the Alps.

BEST RESTAURANTS IN ZERMATT

Surrounded by the majestic Swiss Alps and dominated by the iconic Matterhorn, Zermatt has a diverse gastronomic scene and prides itself on its spectacular scenery. From cozy mountain huts to gourmet restaurants, Zermatt offers a variety of dining options to suit every taste. Here are some of the best restaurants in Zermatt where you can taste the best Swiss and international cuisine:

1. After Seven: After Seven is a Michelin-starred rice restaurant located in the Grand Hotel Zermatt Hof. Chef Ivo Adam creates creative dishes using locally sourced ingredients for modern comfort food.

2. Chez Vrony: Located on the slopes above Zermatt, Chez Vrony is a charming mountain restaurant famous for its traditional Swiss cuisine. Guests can enjoy a hearty meal on the sun terrace with panoramic views of the Matterhorn.

3. The Omnia: Omnia restaurant combines modern design with great food. Focusing on seasonal and local

ingredients, this grand restaurant offers a culinary experience evocative of the Swiss Alps theme.

4. Findlerhof: Findlerhof is a charming restaurant located in the charming village of Zmutt. Known for its cozy atmosphere and unique cuisine, Findlerhof offers Swiss specialties with a focus on quality and originality.

5. Cervo Puro: Cervo Puro is part of Cervo Mountain Resort and is a restaurant in Zermatt. Focusing on local and sustainable products, the restaurant offers fresh dishes reflecting the flavors of the Alps.

6. Sparky's Bar & Restaurant: Sparky's Bar & Restaurant is a popular choice for casual dining. With a wide variety of dishes including burgers, pasta, and international favorites, this

is a great place to enjoy great food and atmosphere.

7. Sonnmatten Restaurant: The Sonnmatten restaurant is located on a high hill and has beautiful views of the surrounding mountains. The menu includes Swiss specialties and the terrace provides a beautiful setting for al fresco dining.

8. Walliserstube Zermatt: Walliserstube Zermatt is located in the Mont Cervin Palace and specializes in traditional Valais cuisine. Its beautiful location, good service, and Swiss classics make it popular with locals and tourists.

9. Hennu Stall: Hennu Stall is a rustic mountain hut serving Swiss cuisine. Accessible via charming walking paths, this hidden gem offers a comfortable environment to enjoy

local specialties such as fondue and raclette.

10. Bäckerei Fuchs: For those with a sweet tooth, Bäckerei Fuchs is a famous restaurant in Zermatt. Carefully selected fresh bread, pastries, and desserts.

11. Le Gitan Grill: Le Gitan Grill is a popular steakhouse in Zermatt, known for its delicious grilled meats and nice atmosphere. The menu includes a selection of prime steaks and other specialty dishes.

12. Papperla Pub: Combining a pub with good food, Papperla Pub is the place to be in the heart of Zermatt. Enjoy Swiss and international cuisine, including burgers, salads, and hearty mountain delicacies.

13. Ristorante Capri: Those who want to taste Italy should go to Ristorante

Capri in Zermatt. This family restaurant offers a menu of authentic Italian dishes, including pasta, pizza, and seafood.

14. Restaurant Julen: Restaurant Julen is part of the Romantik Hotel Julen and offers traditional Swiss cuisine based on local ingredients. The warm and inviting atmosphere adds to the overall dining experience.

15. Schäferstube: The Schäferstube is located in the Schwarzsee Hotel and offers you a cozy and friendly gastronomic atmosphere. The menu combines Swiss and international cuisine, and the terrace restaurant has stunning views of the Matterhorn.

When dining at Zermatt, make a reservation in advance, especially during high season. Whether you want to taste gourmet cuisine, traditional Swiss dishes, or international delicacies, Zermatt's different restaurants allow you to take a pleasant walk among the beautiful Alpine landscape.

COZY CAFÉS AND BAKERIES

With its alpine charm and beautiful scenery, Zermatt has many delightful cafes and bakeries where guests can relax and enjoy delicious food. Whether you're looking for a cup of coffee, a cookie, or a place to relax and enjoy the mountains, Zermatt's cafes and bakeries provide a welcoming environment. Here are some nice places to consider while you're in Zermatt:

1. Café du Pont: Located in the heart of Zermatt, Café du Pont is a charming spot known for its excellent coffee and pastries. The outdoor terrace is the perfect vantage point to admire the picturesque surroundings.

2. Haus Bakery Matthieu: This bakery near Bahnhofstrasse is popular with locals and tourists. Known for its fresh bread, pastries, and sandwiches, Haus Bakery Matthieu is the perfect place for a snack.

3. Mountain Thyme Coffee: If you are a coffee lover, Mountain Thyme Coffee is your best choice. This specialty coffee shop offers expertly brewed coffee in a casual atmosphere. The menu includes different types of coffee beans and brewing methods for those who like to explore.

4. Chez Heini: Chez Heini is a rustic Alpine chalet that combines a traditional Swiss chalet atmosphere with a charming café. Guests can enjoy a variety of beverages, desserts, and snacks in a warm and inviting atmosphere.

5. Café Richemont: Located in the center of Zermatt, Café Richemont is a classic Swiss café with a cozy interior and a menu of various pastries, cakes, and foods. It's the perfect place to relax after a day of exploring.

6. Biner Bäckerei-Café: Biner Bäckerei-Café is a bakery and café offering a wide range of cakes, pastries and cupcakes. The cozy interior and friendly service make this a favorite among locals and tourists.

7. Snowboat Cafe/Bar: For a unique experience, head to Snowboat Cafe/Bar, a boat-like restaurant serving a variety of drinks and snacks. It's interesting design and friendly atmosphere make it a great attraction in Zermatt.

8. Hotel Post Zermatt Café and Bar: Hotel Post Zermatt The hotel's café

and bar provide a relaxing environment to enjoy coffee, cocktails, or dessert. Comfortable seats and good friends make this a great place to relax.

9. Alpenrose Café: Alpenrose Café is conveniently located near the Gornergrat train station and offers a selection of coffee drinks and pastries. This is a convenient stop for those traveling to and from Gornergrat.

10. Bakery & Tea Room Mexico: Bakery & Tea Room Fuchs is a well-known restaurant in Zermatt offering a wide range of delicious desserts, cakes, and teas. Its beautiful venue and delicious food make this place a favorite of dessert lovers.

11. Hotel Monte Rosa - Ruden Bar and Café: Ruden Bar and Café is located in the historic Monte Rosa Hotel and exudes old-world charm. Guests can

enjoy a variety of drinks, pastries, and food in a beautiful setting.

12. Käsestube: Käsestube is a cheese shop and café where you can taste a variety of Swiss cheeses along with local wines. Its relaxed atmosphere makes it a good choice for cheese lovers.

13. Biner's Café and Confiserie: Biner's Café and Confiserie is a restaurant known for its delicious pastries, chocolates, and desserts. The smell of freshly cooked food welcomes visitors to this charming place.

14. Coop supermarket cafe: The Coop supermarket in Zermatt has a cafe where you can grab a quick coffee or snack. For those looking for somewhere relaxing and comfortable, this is an easy choice.

15. Backerei Pollinger: Backerei Pollinger is a restaurant and café with a long tradition in Zermatt. The enchanting aroma of freshly baked bread and cookies invites visitors to taste local delicacies.

Whether you want to start the day with a hot cup of coffee, relax with something sweet, or simply enjoy the Alpine air, Zermatt's cafes and bakeries offer the perfect place to stay to soak in the mountain views.

CHAPTER 8: NIGHTLIFE AND ENTERTAINMENT

BARS AND PUBS

Surrounded by the beautiful Swiss Alps with the iconic Matterhorn in the background, Zermatt has a vibrant nightlife with many bars and pubs. After a day of outdoor adventure or exploring the charming village, visitors can relax and socialize in the relaxed atmosphere of Zermatt's bars and taverns. Here are some popular places to experience Zermatt at night:

1. Brown Cow Pub: Brown Cow Pub is a nice and cozy English-style pub in the center of Zermatt. Known for its nice atmosphere, this is a great place

for a variety of beers, cocktails, and bar food. Live music events add color to nightlife.

2. Papperla Pub: Papperla Pub is located near the Gornergrat train station and is popular with locals and tourists for its park and outdoor terrace.

3. SchneewittchenBar: Located at Hotel Pollux, Schneewittchen Bar is a cozy and comfortable venue known for its creative cocktails and extensive wine list. The relaxed atmosphere makes this place ideal for a relaxing evening.

4. The North Wall Bar: Part of the Hotel Firefly, the North Wall Bar is a vibrant and modern bar where guests can enjoy signature cocktails and sophisticated cuisine. The bar's modern design and mountain views create a unique atmosphere.

5. Cervo Bar: Located at Cervo Mountain Boutique Resort, Cervo Bar is a beautiful venue serving a variety of cocktails and spirits. The bar's terrace offers beautiful views of the Matterhorn and is a popular choice for evening drinks.

6. Snowboat: A Snowboat is a boat-like boat that adds freshness to the Zermatt night. Its location near the Gornergrat train station and its selection of drinking and entertainment venues make it a particularly friendly venue.

7. Hennu Stall Bar: Hennu Stall Bar is part of the Hennu Stall Mountain Lodge and has a nice yet relaxed atmosphere. Enjoy a variety of drinks, including local specialties, in this charming venue that embodies the spirit of the Alps.

8. Hotel Post Zermatt - Broken Bar: Hotel Post Zermatt's Broken Bar is a beautiful place with a modern design. Offering a variety of cocktails and drinks, the restaurant is a stylish place to relax after a day of research.

9. Alex Lounge Bar: Located at the Unique Hotel Post, Alex Lounge Bar is known for its clothes and modernity. Guests can enjoy a variety of cocktails, wines, and spirits in a sophisticated atmosphere.

10. Cervo Cigar Bar: Located at Cervo Mountain Resort, Cervo Cigar Bar is a stylish venue specializing in spirits and creative cocktails. The bar's terrace offers a beautiful view to enjoy a drink under the stars.

11. Harry's Ski Bar: Harry's Ski Bar is a classic ski bar where visitors can enjoy a cozy lounge and a variety of drinks. It is near the Sunnegga lift and

is a favorite with skiers and snowboarders.

12. Mont Cervin Palace - Vernissage Bar: Located in Mont Cervin Palace, Vernissage Bar has a nice atmosphere with live music. This is a sophisticated venue where you can enjoy a cocktail or glass of wine in elegant surroundings.

13. Hotel Riffelhaus - Zirbenstube: The Zirbelstube of the Hotel Riffelhaus is a beautiful retreat with a Swiss atmosphere. Guests can relax by the fireplace and drink a variety of drinks in the beautiful Alpine setting.

14. Hotel Julen - Vernissage: Hotel Julen's Vernissage is a beautiful place with an artistic concept. It has a large selection of cocktails, wines, and spirits, making it a beautiful and cultural place for evenings.

15. Restaurant Julen - Brown Cow Bar: Brown Cow Bar at Restaurant Julen is a cozy and welcoming place to enjoy a drink in a relaxed atmosphere.

The bar's friendly atmosphere makes it a popular choice for conversation. Whether you prefer a classic ski resort, a stylish hotel, or a cozy venue, Zermatt's bars and pubs offer many options for a fun evening on this fascinating mountain.

CULTURAL EVENTS AND FESTIVALS

Surrounded by the majestic Swiss Alps and dominated by the iconic Matterhorn, Zermatt is not only a paradise for outdoor enthusiasts but also the site of many cultural events and festivals throughout the year. These events celebrate the region's rich heritage and allow visitors to immerse themselves in local culture.

Some of the traditions and festivals in Zermatt include

1. Zermatt Unplugged: Zermatt Unplugged is a music festival held every year in April. The festival is famous for its intimate acoustic performances attracting Swiss and international artists. Venues ranging from small tents to large stages in villages offer unique and unforgettable music.

2. Gornergrat Zermatt Marathon: The Gornergrat Zermatt Marathon takes place in July and takes place in St. Niklaus and Gornergrat ends at the train station. The marathon attracts elite runners and participants alike and offers beautiful views of the Matterhorn along the way.

3. Zermatt Music Festival: Zermatt Music Festival is a music festival held every year in August. It brings

together international musicians and musicians to perform in various venues in Zermatt, including churches and open-air venues. A wide repertoire, from classics to contemporary works, is exhibited at the festival.

4. Swiss National Day Celebrations: Swiss National Day, celebrated on 1 August, is a major event across the country, and Zermatt also joins in the celebration. Visitors can enjoy traditional Swiss music, dance performances, fireworks, and many cultural events that create an atmosphere in the village.

5. Zermatt Food Festival - Zermatt Food Festival: Zermatt Food Festival, also known as "Zermatt Food Festival", will be held in September. It is a culinary festival that brings together local chefs, international chefs, and food enthusiasts. The

festival includes artistic performances, tastings, and special events showcasing the many flavors of Zermatt.

6. International Air Show: Zermatt occasionally hosts international air shows with acrobatic demonstrations of pilots. The spectacular air show with the Matterhorn in the background creates a unique and exciting experience for spectators.

7. Zermatt International Film Festival and Awards (ZIFF): The Zermatt International Film Festival and Awards (ZIFF) is an annual event celebrating independent filmmaking. The festival, usually held in September, brings together filmmakers, actors, and cinema lovers from all over the world with a wide selection of films.

8. Swiss Chamber Music Festival: Zermatt Swiss Chamber Music Festival is a classical music festival that takes place in September. It features chamber music performances by famous musicians in intimate venues, allowing visitors to experience the beauty of classical music up close and personal.

9. Wolli's Adventure Park: Wolli's Adventure Park is a family-friendly park for children only. The park, named after Zermatt's mascot Wolli, offers activities, games, and entertainment. It operates during the summer months and aims to create entertainment and education for young visitors.

10. Matterhorn Eagle Cup: The Matterhorn Eagle Cup is an annual golf tournament held at the Matterhorn Golf Club. Golf enthusiasts can participate in this

event while admiring the beautiful mountains surrounding the golf course.

11. Zermatt Fashion Show: Zermatt occasionally hosts fashion shows featuring local and international designers. These events showcase the latest trends in Alpine fashion and provide a platform for new talent.

12. Zermatt Christmas Market: Christmas in Zermatt is celebrated with Christmas celebrations usually held in December. Visitors can enjoy the stunning scenery, buy local products, and taste seasonal dishes against the snow-covered landscape.

These cultural events and festivals contribute to the colorful and diverse nature of Zermatt, allowing visitors to experience local culture, music, art, and cuisine surrounded by the unique beauty of the Swiss Alps.

EVENING STROLLS AND VIEWS

Zermatt, bathed in the glow of the setting sun with the iconic Matterhorn as a backdrop, offers enchanting opportunities for evening strolls that reveal the beauty of this Alpine paradise. The village itself, car-free and brimming with charm, is a delightful place to explore as the day winds down. Here are some recommendations for evening strolls and views in Zermatt:

1. Bahnhofstrasse and Hinterdorf: Begin your evening stroll on Bahnhofstrasse, Zermatt's main street. Lined with shops, cafes, and boutiques, it's a vibrant hub of activity. As you move away from the main street into Hinterdorf, the oldest part of Zermatt, you'll encounter narrow lanes, traditional chalets, and a more serene atmosphere. The lights

of these historical buildings are very beautiful at night.

2. Promenade along the Vespa River: Take a walk along the Vespa River, especially when the sun starts to set. Reflections of the mountain landscape create a picturesque view of the slowly flowing water. Chairs in the gallery are the best place to relax and enjoy the peace.

3. Gornergrat Sunset: Consider taking the Gornergrat Railway to the top of Gornergrat for a spectacular view of the evening glow. As the sun sets behind the mountains, the sky will turn into a canvas of warm tones and the Matterhorn will take on a mesmerizing glow. It was a great experience with a great dinner at Kulm Hotel Gornergrat.

4. Winkelmatten to St. Mauritius Church: Walk from the village to

Winkelmatten, a quiet area of Zermatt. Charming chalets and historic St. Church of Mauritius. The views of the Matterhorn in the distance and the tranquility create a peaceful atmosphere perfect for an evening stroll.

5. Schwarzsee - Stellisee Road: If you want to go for a walk, you can enjoy the beauty of the Matterhorn in the evening along the Schwarzsee - Stellisee road. As day turns to night, the reflection of the mountain peaks in the calm waters of the Stellisee is particularly fascinating.

6. Matter Vispa River Walk: Take a beautiful walk along the Matter Vispa River west of Zermatt. The sound of the river, the surrounding mountain scenery and the dusk in the sky create a peaceful environment.

7. Walks to Leisee: If you want a short walk with beautiful views, consider the path to Leisee. This mountain lake, situated near the Sunnegga funicular station, offers reflections of the surrounding peaks. It's a serene spot to enjoy the evening alpenglow.

8. Riverside Path towards Furi: Take a stroll along the riverside path that leads towards Furi. The path follows the course of the river, offering glimpses of the surrounding mountains. As dusk falls, the soft lighting adds a touch of magic to the landscape.

9. Matterhorn Glacier Paradise: Matterhorn Glacier Paradise is the largest station in Europe and offers beautiful views of the mountains and glaciers. Visit in the afternoon or evening to see the changing colors of the Swiss Alps.

10. Riffelseeweg: The Riffelsee Weg trail is a quiet route to the Riffelsee, a mountain lake with a Matterhorn perspective. The path provides a quiet place for an evening walk among the alpine vegetation.

Always check local sunset times as they may vary from year to year. Whether you choose to walk through the village, hike to a mountain lake, or take the train to the top, the evening walks and views of Zermatt, dedicated to the peace and beauty of hell against the backdrop of the majestic Alps, will satisfy you.

CHAPTER 9: SHOPPING IN ZERMATT

SOUVENIR SHOPS

Located in the Swiss Alps and famous for the iconic Matterhorn, Zermatt has a charming rural atmosphere and a variety of souvenir shops offering guests happy souvenirs. Whether you're looking for Swiss crafts, Alpine-style gifts, or Matterhorn-themed souvenirs, Zermatt's gift shops offer plenty of options to commemorate your beautiful backdrop in the mountains. Here are some souvenir shops in Zermatt:

1. Zermatt Tourist Boutiques: The Zermatt Tourist Office has several shops in the village offering a good selection of souvenirs. From clothing and accessories to traditional Swiss

products, these boutiques are a one-stop shop for tourists looking for authentic gifts.

2. Matterhorn Museum Store: Located at the Matterhorn Museum, the Museum is a treasure trove of Matterhorn-related gifts. You can find books, posters, t-shirts, and exclusive products inspired by Zermatt's rich history and culture and its iconic mountains.

3. Swiss Made Store Zermatt: This store, as the name suggests, specializes in Swiss products. Swiss watches, chocolates, cheeses, and other local crafts are good gifts. Here you can find authentic Swiss gifts to take home.

4. Monte Rosa Hut Shop: If you visit Monte Rosa Hut, which can be reached by cable car, there are many souvenirs and mountain products in

the shop inside the hut. It's a unique opportunity to get souvenirs at a higher altitude.

5. Coop Supermarket: The Coop supermarket in Zermatt has a dedicated section for souvenirs. Here, you can find Swiss chocolates, cheeses, and other local products, making it a convenient stop for both groceries and keepsakes.

6. Schwarzsee Paragliding Shop: If you've experienced paragliding in Zermatt, the Schwarzsee Paragliding Shop near the landing area offers souvenirs related to this thrilling adventure. It's a great place to find items that capture the essence of your paragliding experience.

7. Bäckerei Fuchs Souvenir Shop: Bäckerei Fuchs, a well-known bakery in Zermatt, not only delights visitors with its delicious pastries but also

houses a souvenir shop. Here, you can find Matterhorn-themed chocolates, keychains, and other Alpine-inspired gifts.

8. Swiss Pine: Swiss Pine is a shop specializing in products made from the wood of Swiss stone pine trees. From handcrafted wooden items to aromatic pine pillows, this shop offers unique and locally sourced souvenirs.

9. Edelweiss Zermatt: Edelweiss Zermatt is a boutique that showcases a range of traditional Swiss gifts. The iconic Edelweiss is a symbol of the Alps and features prominently in everything from jewelry to home accessories.

10. Biner Souvenirs: Biner Souvenirs is a store selling various Zermatt and Matterhorn-themed souvenirs. From magnets to postcards, clothing, and

accessories, there is a gift for every taste.

11. Globus Zermatt: Globus is a famous Swiss department store with a branch in Zermatt. The store sells a variety of Swiss and international brands, as well as gifts and souvenirs that showcase Swiss craftsmanship and design.

12. Alphütte Zermatt: Alphütte Zermatt is a store selling a variety of Swiss products. From Swiss watches and knives to rattles and textiles, this store offers a variety of Swiss souvenirs.

13. Riffelalp Resort Store: If you are staying at or visiting Riffelalp Resort, their stores offer unique gifts such as clothing, accessories, and gifts that reflect the luxury of the resort.

14. **Hanni Matterhorn Store:** Hanni Matterhorn Store is a store specializing in Matterhorn-themed products. From Matterhorn-shaped chocolates to unique mountain-inspired gifts, this store represents the essence of Zermatt.

15. **Outdoor Shop:** The Outdoor Shop in Zermatt offers a wide range of outdoor and adventure products. Although it is mostly a shopping mall, it is a good place to find beautiful clothes and accessories that are functional and stylish souvenirs.

Whether you're looking for iconic Matterhorn souvenirs, traditional Swiss crafts, or local products, Zermatt's gourmet shops cater to every taste, allowing you to take home a piece of this Alpine paradise.

LOCAL ARTISANS AND CRAFTS

Located in the heart of the Swiss Alps, Zermatt is famous not only for its spectacular scenery but also for its rich cultural heritage and talented local people who contribute to its local character style. Discover Zermatt's local artisans and masters with the opportunity to find handmade products that reflect Alpine traditions and craftsmanship. Here are some of Zermatt's local workers and crafts:

1. Wood carving: Wood carving is a traditional art of the Swiss Alps, and Zermatt is no exception. Skilled local workers create beautiful designs on wood, creating everything from beautiful objects such as statues and ornaments to practical objects such as vases and furniture. Shades of local woods such as Swiss stone pine are often used in these beautiful pieces.

2. Swiss Rock Pine Product: Swiss Rock Pine (Arve) is a tree species found in the Alps and is valued for its woody aroma. Local craftsmen in Zermatt create many products, including handmade items from Swiss stone pine, pillows filled with essential oils, and pine shavings, known for their beneficial and relaxing properties.

3. Handmade Jewelry: Zermatt's craftsmen draw inspiration from the beautiful surroundings to create unique jewelry. You can find pieces bearing Alpine symbols, such as Edelweiss, or pieces with diamonds that reflect the colors of the landscape. Handmade gold and silver jewelry often appear in local boutiques.

4. Textile Arts: Traditional Swiss textile arts, including embroidery and

sewing, are preserved by local artisans. Beautiful patterns and designs inspired by alpine flora and fauna can be seen in crafts such as tablecloths, scarves, and traditional Swiss clothing such as dresses.

5. Pottery and Ceramics: Local Zermatt potters and ceramic artists create functional and decorative pieces inspired by their Alpine environments. Cups, saucers, and figurines often feature images of mountains, wild animals, and Swiss designs, making them unique and valuable gifts.

6. Alpine cheese: Cheese making is an old tradition in the Swiss Alps and local artisans in Zermatt continue to produce quality Alpine cheese. Visitors can explore the cheese shop and find a variety of cheeses, including the famous raclette and fondue varieties,

often made with milk from the mountains.

7. Felted Wool Products: Zermatt's craftsmen create many products using natural materials, including wool. Handmade products include hats, sandals, and accessories, mostly in Alpine patterns and colors.

8. Leather Products: Zermatt's skilled craftsmen produce leather products such as belts, wallets, and bags. These pieces often feature fine workmanship and durability with Swiss precision.

9. Mountain Photo: A local photographer photographs the beautiful landscape of Zermatt and the surrounding mountains. His works can often be seen in venues and stores, allowing visitors to take home beautiful views.

10. **Alpine Herbal Products:** Zermatt's untouched Alpine environment is a source of inspiration for herbal product artisans. Local shops may sell handmade soaps, creams, and herbs made with ingredients from the surrounding mountains.

11. **Alpine Potpourri and Fragrances:** Zermatt artisans create potpourri and scented products, often using local plants and flowers. These products not only give fragrant gifts but also create the theme of mountain meadows.

12. **Traditional Swiss Watches:** Zermatt is the home of boutiques showcasing Swiss watchmaking craftsmanship. A Swiss watch, although not handmade in a village, is a representation of Swiss precision and craftsmanship.

Visitors to Zermatt can discover these handicrafts and learn about the region's rich heritage by exploring local shops, boutiques, and handicraft workshops. Supporting local artisans not only provides an original and valuable shopping experience but also helps preserve traditional crafts in the heart of the Swiss Alps.

HIGH-END BOUTIQUES

The beautiful Alpine village of Zermatt, below the iconic Matterhorn, is not only a paradise for outdoor enthusiasts but also a beautiful destination. The village is home to high-end boutiques catering to tourists looking for exclusive fashion, Swiss watches, and luxury goods. Here are some luxury stores in Zermatt where you can enjoy great discounts:

1. Bucherer: Bucherer, a famous Swiss retailer, is the destination for luxury watches. The Carl F. Bucherer Zermatt boutique on Bahnhofstrasse displays various famous Swiss watch brands, such as Rolex, Patek Philippe, and Audemars Piguet.

2. Cartier Zermatt: Cartier is a world-famous luxury brand headquartered in Zermatt. The boutique sells a variety of fine jewelry, watches, and accessories renowned for elegance and craftsmanship.

3. Bally: Bally is a luxury Swiss brand that dates back to 1851 and has a store in Zermatt. Known for its quality leather products, including shoes and accessories, Bally offers beautiful and timeless pieces.

4. Moncler: Moncler is a luxury fashion brand known for its jeans, with a boutique in Zermatt. The store

sells stylish and practical winter clothes ideal for the Alps region.

5. Loro Piana: The Italian luxury brand Loro Piana is synonymous with quality cashmere and exclusive fabrics. The Zermatt boutique offers a wide range of beautiful clothes, accessories, and homeware made from the best materials.

6. Hublot Boutique Zermatt: Hublot is a Swiss luxury watch manufacturer with a boutique dedicated to its new watches in Zermatt. Visitors can discover collections that combine modern technology with Swiss watchmaking tradition.

7. Gucci Zermatt: Gucci is an iconic Italian fashion brand with a store in Zermatt. The boutique showcases the latest fashion and accessories that reflect Gucci's signature style and craftsmanship.

8. Omega Boutique: Omega is another famous Swiss watch brand that has a boutique in Zermatt and sells many famous watches. The aim is to recognize its authenticity and participate in important historical events.

9. Hermès Zermatt: Hermès is a luxury French brand known for its craftsmanship and timeless design, with a store in Zermatt. Visitors can explore a wide range of luxury products, including scarves, handbags, and leather goods.

10. Chopard Boutique: Chopard is a Swiss luxury watch and jewelry brand with a branch in Zermatt. The boutique offers a wide range of beautiful watches and jewelry crafted with great attention to detail.

11. Dior Boutique Zermatt: Dior is a famous French fashion house with a boutique in Zermatt where visitors can find the latest haute couture, accessories, and fragrances.

12. Salvatore Ferragamo: Salvatore Ferragamo is a luxury Italian brand known for its shoes and accessories, with a store in Zermatt. The store offers a wide range of stylish and sophisticated products.

13. Brunello Cucinelli: Brunello Cucinelli is an Italian luxury brand specializing in cashmere, with representation in Zermatt. The boutique sells a wide range of elegant clothing and accessories known for their quality and timeless appeal.

14. Rimowa Zermatt: Rimowa is a luxury German brand with a store in Zermatt. Visitors can explore a wide range of high-end products and travel

accessories known for their durability and beautiful designs.

15. Louis Vuitton Zermatt: Louis Vuitton is a French luxury brand that communicates luxury travel and has a branch in Zermatt. The boutique sells a variety of iconic luggage, leather goods, and fashion accessories.

Discover the luxury boutiques in Zermatt and allow visitors to experience luxury shopping against the backdrop of the beautiful Swiss Alps. Whether you're looking for exclusive fashion, Swiss watches, or luxury goods, Zermatt offers the best shopping in a beautiful mountain setting.

CHAPTER 10: WELLNESS AND RELAXATION

SPA AND WELLNESS CENTERS

Zermatt, surrounded by the stunning Swiss Alps and the iconic Matterhorn, offers not only exhilarating outdoor adventures but also opportunities for relaxation and rejuvenation. The village is home to luxurious spa and wellness centers that provide a tranquil escape for visitors seeking pampering and wellness treatments. Here are some notable spa and wellness centers in Zermatt:

1. Mont Cervin Palace – Spa Monte Rosa: The Mont Cervin Palace is a

five-star hotel in Zermatt that features the exquisite Spa Monte Rosa. This spa offers a range of wellness facilities, including indoor and outdoor pools, saunas, steam rooms, and relaxation areas. The spa's ambiance is complemented by stunning views of the Matterhorn.

2. Backstage Hotel Vernissage - Vernissage Spa: Backstage Hotel Vernissage offers art, culture and wellness. Vernissage Spa offers a variety of treatments, from massages to beauty treatments, in a stylish and artistic environment. The spa also includes a sauna, steam room, and relaxation area.

3. Cervo mountain boutique resort - cervo puro spa: Cervo mountain boutique resort offers cervo puro spa, a peaceful retreat with panoramic views of the surrounding mountains. A variety of treatments are offered at

the spa. After a day spent outdoors, guests can relax in the outdoor hot tub or sauna.

4. Riffelalp Resort 2222m - Riffelalp Spa: The Riffelalp Resort, located at an altitude of 2,222 meters, features the Riffelalp Spa with breathtaking views. The spa offers a selection of massages, facials, and wellness treatments, and guests can unwind in the indoor pool or outdoor hot tub.

5. Grand Hotel Zermatterhof - Vita Borni Spa: The Grand Hotel Zermatterhof is an elegant establishment that houses the Vita Borni Spa. This spa provides a serene environment for relaxation and rejuvenation, with facilities such as a Finnish sauna, steam bath, and a range of wellness treatments.

6. Wellness Hotel Alpenhof - Alpenhof Spa: The Wellness Hotel Alpenhof

boasts the Alpenhof Spa, a wellness oasis with a Finnish sauna, bio sauna, steam bath, and relaxation area. Guests can indulge in various massages and beauty treatments in this cozy and inviting environment.

7. Unique Hotel Post - Vita Borni Spa: Unique Hotel Post is home to the Vita Borni Spa, offering a variety of wellness treatments and a rooftop wellness area with stunning views of the Matterhorn. The spa includes a Finnish sauna, steam bath, and relaxation room.

8. Alex Lodge - Private Spa: The Alex Lodge offers an exclusive Private Spa experience, allowing guests to enjoy wellness facilities in a private setting. This intimate spa experience includes a sauna, steam room, whirlpool, and relaxation area.

9. Riffelhaus 1853 – Riffelhaus Spa: Riffelhaus 1853, one of the oldest mountain hotels in Zermatt, features the Riffelhaus Spa. Guests can unwind in the sauna or enjoy a massage while taking in panoramic views of the Matterhorn.

10. Hotel Firefly – The Omnia – The Peak Health Club & Spa: The Peak Health Club & Spa at Hotel Firefly – The Omnia offers a luxurious spa experience with a range of treatments and wellness facilities. The spa includes an indoor pool, sauna, and relaxation areas.

11. Schloss Hotel – Vita Borni Spa: The Schloss Hotel is home to the Vita Borni Spa, where guests can indulge in wellness treatments and enjoy the spa facilities. The tranquil environment adds to the overall relaxing experience.

12. Adler Hitta - Adler Spa: Adler Hitta is a charming mountain with its Adler Spa. Guests can enjoy health treatments and enjoy mountain views from the outdoor hot tub and terrace.

The spa and wellness centers at Zermatt offer the perfect workout for those who want to relax and pamper themselves with beautiful Alpine views. Whether it's a relaxing massage, a facial, or a quiet time in the sauna, Zermatt's spa services appeal to those seeking relaxation and beauty in the heart of the Swiss Alps.

YOGA AND MEDITATION

Surrounded by the majestic Swiss Alps and the iconic Matterhorn, Zermatt offers a beautiful setting for those seeking moments of peace, mindfulness, and self-discovery. While the destination is best known for its outdoor adventures, it also offers yoga and meditation opportunities, allowing guests to connect with the beauty of their surroundings. Here are some ways to practice yoga and meditation in Zermatt:

1. Yoga Retreats and Workshops: Zermatt offers many yoga retreats and workshops throughout the year to meet the needs of practitioners of all levels. These events often take advantage of beautiful mountain scenery to provide a unique and inspiring setting for yoga classes. Check the list of local events or work with health centers and daycares to plan a trip.

2. Wellness Hotels and Spas: Many of Zermatt's luxury hotels and spas include yoga and meditation in their services. Guests can attend group lessons with experienced instructors or choose private lessons. These apps

are often designed to promote relaxation and awareness in backcountry areas.

3. Outdoor Yoga: Zermatt's natural surroundings are home to beautiful outdoor yoga studios. Some hotels and health centers offer outdoor yoga classes, allowing participants to practice asanas and meditation while enjoying the fresh mountain air and views of the Swiss Alps.

4. Private Yoga Lessons: Consider booking a private yoga lesson with a local instructor who knows Zermatt's unique atmosphere. This personal approach allows practitioners to tailor their practice to their specific needs and experience the benefits of yoga in an individual setting.

5. Mountain Meditation: Zermatt's mountain trails and peaceful surroundings provide the perfect

environment for meditation. Whether it's a meditation practice or a self-awareness session, the serenity of the mountain creates a wonderful place for understanding and relaxation.

6. Health Retreats: Some health and fitness centers in Zermatt offer packages combining yoga and meditation with spa treatments and outdoor activities. These resorts aim to offer a comprehensive and exhilarating experience in the heart of the Swiss Alps.

7. Zermatt Yoga Studios: Find a local yoga studio in Zermatt that offers regular classes and workshops. These studios will have experienced instructors teaching practitioners in a variety of yoga styles, including hatha, vinyasa, and restorative practices.

8. Awareness Walk: Go on an awareness walk that combines the benefits of walking with awareness. These walks often stop for meditation, allowing participants to connect with nature and experience the present moment in the mountain environment.

9. Yoga and Ski Center (Winter): Zermatt becomes a popular destination for ski enthusiasts during the winter months. Some health centers organize special yoga and ski centers that combine the joy of winter sports with yoga and meditation practices.

10. Yoga and Wellness Events: For special yoga and wellness events in Zermatt, please check local events. These events will include yoga festivals, workshops, and wellness visits conducted by local healers or international instructors.

Before participating in yoga and meditation at Zermatt, it is recommended to check with the local health center, park, or parks for new opportunities and activities. Whether you are an experienced yogi or a beginner interested in the benefits of mindfulness, Zermatt offers you the tranquility and inspiration to explore these practices in the beautiful Swiss Alps.

HOT SPRINGS AND THERMAL BATHS

While Zermatt may not be known for its village spas and spas, Switzerland's surroundings offer many options for those looking for a relaxing holiday in healing waters. The mountain scenery combined with the tranquility of the Swiss Alps provides a peaceful environment to enjoy thermal springs and hot baths.

Here are some famous hot springs and thermal baths accessible from Zermatt:

1. Thermal Bath (Brigerbad): Brigerbad has the best location in the town of Brig. in Switzerland. Brigerbad has several swimming pools, as well as indoor and outdoor thermal pools, allowing visitors to relax and enjoy the views of the surrounding mountains. The thermal water here is rich in minerals and known for its healing properties.

2. Leukerbad Therme (Leukerbad): Leukerbad is in the canton of Valais and is famous for its thermal baths. Leukerbad Therme is one of the most famous health resorts and spa centers in the region. Visitors can enjoy the warm water while enjoying the beautiful Alpine scenery. The building has outdoor and indoor swimming

pools, saunas, and various health facilities.

3. Scuol: Scuol is located in the Engadine region and is famous for its hot mineral water. The Scuol Spa offers a unique bathing experience with its Roman-Irish bath, a sequence of thermal pools, and steam rooms. The waters are sourced from the local mineral springs and are believed to have healing properties.

4. Vals Thermal Baths (Vals): Although a bit farther from Zermatt, the Vals Thermal Baths in the canton of Graubünden are renowned for their architectural and natural beauty. Designed by architect Peter Zumthor, the thermal baths are fed by the Valser Quartzite thermal spring, creating a tranquil and meditative atmosphere for visitors.

5. Ovronnaz Thermal Baths (Ovronnaz): Ovronnaz, located in the Valais region, is known for its thermal baths with panoramic views of the Rhône Valley. The Ovronnaz Thermal Baths offer a range of pools with varying temperatures, as well as saunas and wellness facilities.

The water is sourced from nearby thermal springs. While Zermatt itself may not have hot springs, these nearby thermal baths provide an opportunity for visitors to enjoy the therapeutic benefits of warm, mineral-rich waters against the backdrop of the Swiss Alps. It's recommended to check the opening hours, facilities, and any specific health guidelines or regulations before planning a visit to these thermal baths.

CHAPTER 11: DAY TRIPS FROM ZERMATT

GORNERGRAT RAILWAY

The Gornergrat Railway is a historic cogwheel train that provides a spectacular journey from Zermatt to the summit of Gornergrat, one of the most iconic viewpoints in the Swiss Alps. Offering breathtaking panoramic views of the surrounding mountains, including the majestic Matterhorn, the Gornergrat Railway is a must-visit attraction for both nature enthusiasts and railway aficionados. Here's a closer look at this remarkable railway experience:

Overview:

1. Inauguration: The Gornergrat Railway was inaugurated in 1898,

making it one of the oldest cogwheel railways in Switzerland. Its purpose was to connect Zermatt with the Gornergrat Ridge, providing visitors with access to unparalleled views of the Alps.

2. Cogwheel Technology: The Gornergrat Railway employs a cogwheel system, which allows the train to ascend and descend steep inclines with precision and safety. These machines provide a competitive and comfortable ride on the mountain.

3. Scenic Route: The railway is approximately 9 kilometers (about 5.6 miles) long and reaches the top of the Gornergrat at an altitude of 3,089 meters (10,135 feet). The road takes riders through mountainous landscapes, lush meadows, and lush forests, revealing an ever-changing landscape.

The main stop on Route:

1. Zermatt (1,604 meters): The route starts in Zermatt, a car-free village near the foot of the Matterhorn. Passengers board the cog train at Zermatt train station.

2. Riffelalp (2,211 meters): As the train ascends, it stops at Riffelalp, a picturesque mountain hamlet. This intermediate station offers stunning views and is an ideal starting point for hikers.

3. Riffelberg (2,582 meters): Another stop on the way to Gornergrat, Riffelberg provides breathtaking views of the Gorner Glacier and surrounding peaks. It's a popular spot for hiking and winter sports.

4. Rotenboden (2,815 meters): Rotenboden is known for its

impressive panorama of the Matterhorn. It serves as a starting point for the popular Gornergrat–Riffelsee–Rotenboden hiking trail.

5. Gornergrat Summit (3,089 meters): The journey culminates at the Gornergrat summit, offering one of the most stunning panoramic views in the Alps. Passengers are treated to a 360-degree spectacle of snow-capped peaks, including the Matterhorn, Monte Rosa, and more.

Attractions at Gornergrat Summit:

1. Observatory and Kulmhotel Gornergrat: The Gornergrat Summit features an observatory, allowing visitors to marvel at the clear mountain skies. Kulmhotel Gornergrat, situated at the summit, provides dining facilities, a terrace, and accommodations for those wishing to extend their stay.

2. Panoramic Platforms: Various panoramic platforms and viewing areas are strategically positioned to provide different perspectives of the surrounding peaks. These platforms offer excellent opportunities for photography and enjoying the alpine scenery.

3. Gornergrat Bahn Museum: At the Gornergrat summit, there's a small museum showcasing the history and development of the Gornergrat Railway. It provides insights into the engineering marvels that made this scenic railway possible.

Travel Tips:

1. Timings and Seasonality: The Gornergrat Railway operates year-round. It is particularly popular in both winter and summer, offering different but equally captivating

views. Check the schedule and consider making reservations, especially during peak tourist seasons.

2. Sunrise and Sunset Trips: Sunrise and sunset trips are highly recommended for photographers and those seeking a magical experience. Witnessing the first light of day or the warm hues of sunset against the snow-capped peaks is truly extraordinary.

3. Hiking Opportunities: The Gornergrat area offers a network of hiking trails catering to various skill levels. Hiking enthusiasts can explore trails that lead to neighboring peaks and scenic spots.

4. Combined Tickets: Consider purchasing combined tickets that include the Gornergrat Railway journey along with other attractions

or activities in the region, offering a comprehensive experience.

The Gornergrat Railway stands as a testament to Swiss engineering prowess, offering a journey that is not merely transportation but a captivating experience in itself. The combination of the historic railway, stunning alpine landscapes, and unparalleled views from the Gornergrat summit make this excursion a highlight of any visit to Zermatt.

ZERMATT TO CERVINIA (ITALY)

The journey from Zermatt to Cervinia, Italy is a cross-border adventure that allows travelers to experience the beauty of Switzerland and Italy while surrounded by the stunning Alps. This route combines train travel with a beautiful view, offering beautiful views of the iconic peak and mountain landscape. Here is the journey guide from Zermatt to Cervinia:

Route Overview:

1. Zermatt to Täsch: Start your journey in Zermatt, the car-free Alpine village of the Matterhorn at the foot of the peak. It's a short train ride from Zermatt to Täsch, the last point reached by private vehicle.

2. Täsch to Visp: Take the regional train   Täsch to Visp. Visp is a major transportation hub in the Valais region, connecting various train routes.

3. Visp to Domodossola (Italy):   From Visp, take a scenic train ride to Domodossola, Italy. This part of the journey offers picturesque views as the train winds through the Alps.

4. Domodossola to Milan: In Domodossola, you'll transfer to a train heading to Milan. Milan is a major city with excellent transportation links, making it a convenient stopover.

5. Milan to Turin: From Milan, take the train to Turin (Turin), another major city in northern Italy. This trip allows you to experience the different types of landscapes of northern Italy.

6. Turin to Chatillon: The continues its journey from Turin to Chatillon (a small town in the Aosta Valley region of Italy).

7. Chatillon to Cervinia: From Chatillon, you can take a regional train or bus to reach the fascinating mountain of Cervinia. This small town is located at the foot of the Matterhorn on the Italian side. Cervinia is famous for its excellent

skiing opportunities and magnificent Alpine scenery.

Travel Tips:

1. Train Tickets: It's advisable to check the train schedules and book tickets in advance, especially during peak travel seasons. Ticket prices may vary based on the class of service and availability.

2. Connection Times: Be mindful of connection times between trains. While the Swiss and Italian rail networks are generally punctual, it's wise to have some buffer time, especially when transferring from one train to another.

3. Scenic Views: The train journey between Zermatt and Domodossola is particularly scenic, offering panoramic views of the Alps. Keep

your camera ready to capture the stunning landscapes along the way.

4. Crossing the Border: There are no border controls when traveling by train between Zermatt and Cervinia, as both Switzerland and Italy are part of the Schengen Area. Enjoy the seamless journey across borders.

5. Skiing and Outdoor Activities: Cervinia is a popular destination for skiing and other outdoor activities. If you're visiting in the winter, consider bringing your ski gear to explore the slopes.

6. Weather Alert: Weather may affect the train season, especially in mountainous areas. Check weather and train conditions before departure.

7. Ticket Flexibility: Travel plans are subject to unforeseen changes, so

consider purchasing a transfer ticket or a ticket that allows changes.

The journey from Zermatt to Cervinia is the perfect combination of Swiss train travel and the charm of the Italian countryside. This is an opportunity to experience the different cultures, languages , and landscapes of the Alpine region. Whether you're a nature enthusiast, a skiing aficionado, or simply a traveler seeking scenic beauty, this cross-border journey is sure to leave you with lasting memories.

ZERMATT TO ZERMATT VALLEY

The journey from Zermatt to the Zermatt Valley is a beautiful adventure in the heart of the Swiss Alps, allowing visitors to immerse themselves in the beautiful scenery. The Zermatt Valley, commonly known as Mattertal, covers the surroundings of the village of Zermatt and offers many outdoor activities and spectacular views. Here is a map to explore the Zermatt Valley:

Route Overview:

1. Zermatt Village: Begin your journey to Zermatt, a car-free location near the foot of the iconic Matterhorn village. Zermatt is known for its Alpine charm and chalets and as the gateway to some of the highest peaks in the Swiss Alps.

2. Gornergrat Railway: For panoramic views, consider taking the Gornergrat Railway to the top of Gornergrat Mountain. This historic train offers unique views of the Matterhorn and the surrounding landscape. The route includes stops in Riffelalp, Riffelberg, and Rotenboden, each with a unique view.

3. Hiking in the Zermatt Valley: The Zermatt Valley is a hiker's paradise, with a network of trails suitable for all skill levels. Explore trails like the Five Lakes Trail or the Gorner Gorge Trail to get up close to alpine vistas, glacier lagoons, and waterfalls.

4. Schwarzsee (Black Lake):   For a more challenging hike, consider Schwarzsee, a beautiful alpine lake surrounded by the highest mountains. The Schwarzsee Trail offers beautiful walks on the Matterhorn and surrounding glaciers.

5. Furi and Zmutt: Walk or drive to Furi, a small village above Zermatt. From Furi, you can walk to the charming village of Zmutt, known for its traditional Swiss architecture and surroundings.

6. Hike to Hörnli Hut: Experienced hikers might consider hiking to Hörnli Hut, the base camp for those attempting to complete the Matterhorn. This trail offers beautiful views of the iconic mountain.

7. Valley Mountain Bike: Zermatt Valley offers fun mountain biking for beginners and advanced riders alike. Cycling through alpine meadows, dense forests, and awe-inspiring panoramic views.

Tips for Exploring the Zermatt Valley:

1. Tour Guides: Consider joining a guided tour or hiring a local guide to explore the Zermatt Valley. The guide provides information about the fauna, flora, and geological features of the region.

2. Gondola and Gondolas: Reach the heights quickly with gondolas and

cable cars. This allows you to visit many places and have a different experience in the Zermatt Valley.

3. Seasonal Activities: The Community Center offers many events depending on the season. You can enjoy skiing and snowboarding in the winter months, and make time for hiking, cycling, and mountain trips in the summer months.

4. Alpine Huts and Restaurants: Discover alpine huts and mountain restaurants along the way. These places offer the opportunity to relax, taste local cuisine, and enjoy the hospitality of the Swiss Alps.

5. Photo Opportunities: The Zermatt Valley is a paradise for photographers. Discover the changing colors of the landscape, reflections in alpine lakes, and the play of light and shadow on mountain peaks.

6. Weather Alert: Check the weather forecast before starting a hike or outdoor activity. Weather in the Alps is unpredictable, so it's important to be prepared for change.

7. respect for nature: respect nature and wildlife and practice responsible tourism. Follow the chosen route and follow the "leave no trace" rule to help preserve the pristine mountain environment.

Discover the Zermatt Valley, a pleasant walk through alpine meadows, glacial lakes, and high peaks. Whether you are an outdoor enthusiast, a nature lover, or a tranquility seeker, the Zermatt Valley offers an unforgettable experience in the heart of the Swiss Alps.

CHAPTER 12: PRACTICAL INFORMATION

LANGUAGE AND CURRENCY

Languages in Zermatt:

Zermatt's mountain dialects reflect many languages of Switzerland. The village is located in the German-speaking part of the country, specifically in the canton of Valais (Wallis in German). Therefore, the main language in Zermatt is Swiss German. However, due to its international appeal and tourist diversity, English is widely understood and used in hotels, restaurants, and related businesses. In addition, French and Italian are languages that show the linguistic diversity of Switzerland. Here is a summary of the languages you may encounter in Zermatt:

1. Swiss German (Schweizerdeutsch): Locals and Swiss Germans often communicate in Alemannic German. Although it is different from the German model, most residents are quite familiar with both models.

2. English: English is widely spoken, especially in the business world. You'll find that hotel staff, restaurant staff, and tour guides mostly speak English.

3. French: Since Zermatt is located in the French-speaking town of Valais, you will meet French-speaking people, especially in management and the office.

4. Italian: Due to its proximity to the Italian-speaking part of Switzerland and Zermatt's international appeal, you can meet Italian speakers.

Zermatt Currency:

Switzerland's currency, Zermatt, is based on the Swiss Franc (CHF). Some important facts about the currency of Zermatt:

1. Swiss Franc (CHF): The currency of Zermatt is the Swiss Franc. Currencies include coins (laptops) and banknotes (francs). Credit and debit cards are widely accepted, but it is recommended that you bring some cash, especially for small businesses.

2. Credit and Debit Cards: Major credit and debit cards such as Visa, MasterCard, and American Express are widely accepted at hotels, restaurants, stores, and other

businesses. But it's a good idea to check ahead of time, especially in more remote or smaller areas.

3. ATMs: ATMs (Automatic Teller Machines) are widely available in Zermatt and allow tourists to withdraw Swiss Francs. Please check with your bank about international withdrawal fees.

4. Currency Exchange: Banks, exchange offices, and some hotels offer currency exchange services. It is recommended to compare exchange rates before exchanging money.

5. Tipping: Tipping is customary in Switzerland, but not mandatory. At restaurants, most service charges are included in the bill. However, to receive good service, it is necessary to either do all of them or give up the idea.

6. Currency decision: Switzerland is not part of the European Union and the euro is not a currency. Although some businesses accept Euros, it is recommended to do business in Swiss Francs.

Understanding Zermatt's powerful language and competitive advantages will ensure a more enjoyable, more enjoyable experience during your visit. Whether you're walking the village's charming streets, interacting with locals, or making business deals, understanding these factors will enhance your stay in this jewel of the Alps.

EMERGENCY INFORMATION

Although Zermatt is a safe and well-managed destination, it is important to know emergency information to ensure your safety and well-being. Here is a guide to emergency services, medical facilities, and safety advice in Zermatt:

Emergency Services:

1. Emergency Number: The emergency number for Switzerland (e.g. Zermatt) is 112. This number can help you call emergency police, medical services, and emergency services. fire services.

2. Police: In non-emergency situations, you can contact your local police station. Zermatt police phone number: +41 27 966 69 00.

3. Emergency Medical: If there is an emergency, call 112 or go to the nearest health center. Hôpital de Zermatt (Zermatt Hospital) is located in the village and can provide medical assistance.

4. Mountain Rescue: Zermatt is a popular destination for outdoor activities such as hiking and skiing. In case of an emergency in the mountains, please call the Zermatt Air Rescue Service on +41 27 966 89 00.

Medical facilities:

1. Hôpital de Zermatt (Zermatt Hospital):
  - Address: Hofmattstrasse 4, 3920 Zerm
  - Telephone: + 41 27 966 41 11

2. Pharmacies: Many places where you can buy medicines and get advice on minor health problems There is a pharmacy.

2. Dentist: If you have a dental emergency, you can contact your local dentist for help.

Safety Instructions:

1. Altitude Warnings: Zermatt is at a high altitude. If you are sensitive to altitude or have a pre-existing condition, please consult a doctor before visiting.

2. Weather Awareness: Weather in the Alps can change quickly. Check the weather forecast before embarking on outdoor activities and be prepared for sudden changes in temperature and visibility.

3. Mountain Safety: If you are participating in mountain activities such as hiking or skiing, explain your plan to others, bring the necessary equipment, and learn to walk. Be aware of road closures and follow safety instructions.

4. Skiing and Winter Sports: If you participate in winter sports, follow safety rules, use appropriate

equipment, and be aware of current avalanche risks. Follow local government guidelines.

5. Travel Insurance: Make sure you have travel insurance that covers emergencies, evacuations, and other unforeseen events.

6. COVID-19 Guide: Stay up to date with the latest advice and restrictions on COVID-19. Follow local health regulations and follow safety precautions.

7. Local Information: Find the location of emergency services, medical facilities, and nearest residence.

8. Lost Property: If you have lost your property or information, please contact local police or authorities.

By knowing the emergency services, being aware of your surroundings, and taking the necessary precautions, you can enjoy your time in Zermatt by staying safe and secure in this beautiful Alpine environment.

USEFUL CONTACTS

Having a key contact person for information, assistance and emergencies is essential when visiting Zermatt. List of useful contact information in Zermatt:

Emergency Response:

1. Emergency Services:
   - Emergency Number: 112 This number helps you call emergency services, including police, medical assistance, and fire protection.

2. Zermatt Police:

- Tel: +41 27 966 69 00 In non-emergency situations you can contact your local station.

3. Air Zermatt (Mountain Rescue):
 - Tel: +41 27 966 89 00 In the event of an emergency while working in the mountains, especially outdoors, please contact Air Zermatt for rescue assistance.

Medical contact:

1. Hôpital de Zermatt:
 - Address: Hofmattstrasse 4, 3920 Zermatt, Switzerland
 - Phone: +41 27 966 41 11

2. Home Medicine: If you have minor health concerns or need over-the-counter medications, visit your local pharmacy.

3. Dentist: For dental emergencies, please contact your local dentist.

Transportation:

1. Zermatt Train Station:
   - Zermatt Train Station is the main transportation hub.
   - Information: +41 27 966 01 01

2. Gornergrat Railway:
   - Information about the Gornergrat Railway.
   - Tel: +41 27 927 77 00 Zermatt

3. Taxi Service:
   - Taxi services are available locally.
   - You can get the number from your address or the train station.

Tourist Information:

1. Zermatt Tourist Office:

- For general information, maps and services.
- Address: Bahnhofplatz 5, 3920 Zermatt, Switzerland Phone: +41 27 966 81 00

2. Mountain Guides and Tours:
- For guided tours and outdoor activities, please contact your local guide.

Accomodation:

1. Your reception:
- The reception desk at your hotel or accommodation is a great source of local information and assistance.

Lost and Found Items:

1. Zermatt Police (lost items):
- In case of loss of items or documents.

- Phone: +41 27 966 69 00
COVID-19

COVID-19 information:

1. Local Health Department:
   - Stay informed about the latest advice and restrictions regarding COVID-19.

Other useful contacts:

1. Swiss Post Office:
   - is located in Zermatt and provides postal services.
   - Address: Bahnhofplatz, 3920

2. Zermatt Clearing:
   - For clearing services. can be purchased from banks and exchange offices.

3. Internet and mobile service:

- Please contact your home or local Internet and mobile service provider.

4. Zermatt Environmental Office:
    - Information on sustainable practices. Phone: +41 27 967 68 30

Having these contacts provides easy access to help, information, and services during your stay in Zermatt. Whether you need medical attention, transportation, or guidance on local attractions, these connections will help make your experience in this charming Alpine village enjoyable and comfortable.

CHAPTER 13: SUSTAINABILITY IN ZERMATT

ECO-FRIENDLY PRACTICES

Surrounded by the untouched beauty of the Swiss Alps, Zermatt is committed to promoting a healthy and safe lifestyle. Zermatt, a car-free village at the foot of the iconic Matterhorn, takes environmental protection and responsible tourism seriously. Some good environmental practices and initiatives in Zermatt are

Car-free villages:

1. No cars allowed: Zermatt is a car-free village where only electric taxis and horse-drawn carriages are allowed. This not only reduces pollution but also helps create a quieter, more peaceful environment.

Renewable energy:

1. Hydropower: Switzerland is known for its abundance of clean energy. Zermatt also reduces its carbon footprint by using electricity.

Waste management:

1. waste separation: Zermatt promotes waste separation to facilitate the disposal of recyclables by residents and visitors. There are bins for glass, paper, and other recyclable materials throughout the village.

2. Don't litter: Signs and campaigns promoting the importance of littering.

Guests are encouraged to respect nature by disposing of garbage.

Sustainable transportation:

1. Electric taxi: Electric taxi is the main form of transportation in the village. This not only reduces air pollution and noise but is also in line with Switzerland's commitment to mobility.

2. Main Transportation: residents and visitors have good access to public transportation, including trains and cable cars. This encourages the use of eco-friendly travel for trips and excursions.

Environmental Education:

1. Zermatt Environmental Office: Zermatt Environmental Office cooperates on cultural promotion. They provide information and

resources to residents, businesses, and visitors, encouraging a collective effort for environmental preservation. Sustainable Accommodations:

2. Certified Green Hotels: Many accommodations in Zermatt are committed to sustainable tourism. Some hotels have received certifications for their eco-friendly practices, such as energy efficiency and waste reduction.

Responsible Tourism:

1. Leave No Trace: Visitors are encouraged to follow the "Leave No Trace" principles. This involves respecting natural landscapes, staying on designated paths, and minimizing any impact on the environment.

2. Nature Conservancy: Zermatt cooperates with the nature conservancy. This includes measures

to protect mountain ecosystems as well as local flora and fauna.

Regenerative Building Practice:

1. Energy Efficient Building: New construction and renovation often include energy-efficient technologies and contribute to the sustainability of the village.

Sustainability Events:

1. Eco-Friendly Events: Zermatt hosts sustainability-focused events. These activities often include measures to reduce waste, encourage recycling, and raise awareness of environmental issues.

Community Involvement:

1. Community Gardens: Zermatt supports community gardens that raise awareness of community

sustainability and encourage residents to grow their gardens.

2. Local Initiatives: Local businesses and residents have created a shared commitment to sustainable development by partnering with leaders who support environmental stewardship.

Zermatt is committed to environmentally friendly practices that are in line with Switzerland's overall commitment to caring for the environment. Whether admiring the beautiful landscapes, exploring the village, or participating in outdoor activities, Zermatt offers an example of tourism and living in harmony with nature.

RESPONSIBLE TOURISM INITIATIVES

Surrounded by the breathtaking beauty of the Swiss Alps and home to the iconic Matterhorn, Zermatt is committed to responsible tourism. The village is aware of the importance of preserving its natural and cultural heritage while providing visitors with a good and beneficial experience. Here is some responsible tourism in Zermatt:

Sustainable transportation:

1. Car-free village: Zermatt is a car-free village that reduces pollution and creates a peaceful environment. Encourage the use of electric taxis, horse-drawn carriages, and good public transport options.

2. Electric transportation: The widespread use of electric taxis and

buses helps reduce carbon emissions. The village encourages the use of clean and sustainable transportation methods.

Eco-friendly accommodation:

1. Green certification: Some hotels in Zermatt have received a green certificate, demonstrating their commitment to sustainable and responsible operations. These products use energy-saving measures and waste-reduction strategies.

Garbage:

1. Recycling Initiative: Zermatt actively supports waste sorting and recycling. Visitors will see clear signs encouraging responsible disposal of different types of waste.

2. Litter Prevention Campaign: The village is running a campaign to raise

awareness about the importance of not littering. Guests are encouraged to respect nature and dispose of waste.

Nature Conservancy:

1. Alpine Conservation Project: Zermatt participates in projects for the protection of the mountain environment. This includes protecting local flora and fauna, protecting natural habitats, and promoting biodiversity.

2. Road Protection: The responsibility of the tourism sector includes the management and protection of the road. Visitors are encouraged to stay on track to minimize the impact on fragile mountain ecosystems.

Education and Information:

1. Zermatt Environmental Office: The Zermatt Environmental Office plays an important role in supporting responsible tourism. They provide cultural and environmental preservation information to visitors, businesses, and residents.

2. Educational Guide: Information guides throughout the village and at major attractions educate visitors about the local environment, wildlife, and the importance of good manners.

Community involvement in the community:

1. Community gardens: Zermatt promotes community gardens to improve sustainability awareness in the community. Residents and visitors can participate in or learn from community programs.

2. Local artisans and artisans: Encourage visitors to support local artisans and artisans to help preserve culture and value tourism in the community.

Responsible Events:

1. Best Practices: Events in Zermatt often include sustainable practices. Measures will include reducing waste, recycling, and using environmentally friendly products.

Ethical Wildlife Tourism:

1. Responsible Wildlife: Zermatt tour operators attach importance to the responsible monitoring of wildlife. Top tips minimize impact on local animals and care for their habitat.

Community Cooperation:

1. Cooperation with NGOs: Zermatt cooperates with non-governmental organizations (NGOs) focusing on environmental protection and tourism control.

2. Collaboration with local businesses: Encouraging local businesses to adopt responsible practices, such as reducing single-use plastics or sustainable products, contributes to full-service tourism.

Sports and Arts:

1. Cultural Sensitivity: Guests are encouraged to respect local culture. Understanding and appreciating local culture and traditions can promote tourism while promoting cultural preservation.

3. Eco Tours: Tours focused on environmental education provide visitors with a deeper understanding

of local ecosystems and the importance of protecting nature.

Zermatt's commitment to responsible tourism not only preserves the natural beauty of the region but also ensures the development of the community and its unique culture. Visitors to Zermatt are encouraged to take advantage of these plans so that they can make a positive contribution to the conservation of this Alpine paradise.

CHAPTER 14: CONCLUSION

MEMORABLE EXPERIENCES

Located in the Swiss Alps with the iconic Matterhorn in the background, Zermatt offers unforgettable experiences to its visitors. Whether you're an outdoor enthusiast, a nature lover, or someone looking for cultural inspiration, Zermatt has something to offer. Here are some unforgettable experiences that will make your time in Zermatt special:

1. Matterhorn Panorama: Witnessing the sunrise or sunset from the Matterhorn is an unforgettable experience. Head to viewpoints like

Gornergrat or Schwarzsee, where the changing colors of the sky illuminate the highest mountains.

2. Gornergrat Railway tour: Take a guided tour of the Gornergrat Railway. The cog train ride offers panoramic views of the Alps and leads to the breathtaking Matterhorn panorama from the top of Gornergrat.

3. Hiking Trails: Discover Zermatt's extensive hiking trails. There are trails for all skill levels, from hikes to challenging hikes. The Five Lakes Trail and Thornley Hut Trail are particularly memorable.

4. Skiing or snowboarding: During the winter months, you can experience the excitement of skiing or snowboarding in the Zermatt-Cervinia Ski Area. With its stunning mountain views and well-groomed

slopes, it is a paradise for winter sports.

5. Matterhorn Glacier Paradise: Visit Matterhorn Glacier Paradise, Europe's largest ski resort. Marvel at breathtaking views, explore the Ice Palace and experience the thrill of standing on a glacier.

6. Paragliding in the Alps: Enjoy paragliding. Soar above the Zermatt Valley and enjoy panoramic views of the surrounding area for an exhilarating experience.

7. Zermatt Village Walk: Walk through the pedestrianized streets of Zermatt. Enjoy traditional wooden huts, explore charming streets, and discover local shops and cafes.

8. Mountain Bike Adventure: Explore mountain terrain on a mountain bike. Zermatt offers a variety of hikes

suitable for different skill levels, offering an exciting way to experience this beautiful landscape.

9. Beautiful views and delicious food: Enjoy delicious food with the Matterhorn in the background. Many restaurants have dining rooms with terraces, providing the perfect setting for a memorable meal.

10. Cultural events and festivals: Immerse yourself in Zermatt culture by attending local events and festivals. From traditional festivals to music festivals, these events showcase the beauty of local culture.

11. Stellisee Reflection: Hike to Stellisee, a pristine mountain lake that reflects the Matterhorn. Take amazing photos as the iconic view is reflected in the river.

12. Zermatt Railway Adventure: Explore the region by train, including the Gornergrat Railway and the spectacular Glacier Express. The journey itself becomes an unforgettable part of your Zermatt experience.

13. Health & Spa: - Relax and unwind at one of Zermatt's health resorts and spas. After a day of outdoor adventure, you can reward yourself at a mountain resort.

14. Night View: - The magic of Zermatt under the night sky. Join the stargazing show and see the stars and the Milky Way in the fresh air of the Alps.

15. Christmas in Zermatt: - Zermatt will be decked out in Christmas lights if you visit during the festive season. The village exudes magic and the festival markets offer local crafts and food.

Zermatt's appeal lies not only in its stunning views but also in the many activities and experiences it offers. Whether you're looking for adventure, relaxation, or cultural immersion, Zermatt ensures that every moment becomes a precious memory.

PLANNING YOUR NEXT VISIT

Planning your next visit to Zermatt, the picturesque Alpine village at the base of the iconic Matterhorn, involves considering various aspects to ensure a seamless and enjoyable experience. Here's a comprehensive guide to help you plan your trip:

1. Choose the Right Time to Visit: Zermatt is a year-round destination. Winter is perfect for skiing and snow activities, while summer offers hiking

and outdoor adventures. Consider your preferred activities and weather conditions when planning.

2. Length of stay: Decide how long you want to stay in Zermatt. The village and its surroundings have many activities, so take advantage of the time that allows you to explore from a comfortable place.

3. Address: First, call and write the address. There are many options in Zermatt, from cozy chalets to luxury hotels. Imagine being in the middle of a car-free city for easy access to attractions.

4. Transportation: Arrange transportation to Zermatt. Since the village is closed to cars, you need to take a train or taxi from the nearest public transportation. The train ride to Zermatt is nice and easy.

5. Budgets and Expenses: Create a travel budget that includes accommodations, meals, activities, and transportation. Zermatt may be a beautiful place, but there are options for every budget.

6. Travel Insurance: Ensure you have comprehensive travel insurance covering medical emergencies, trip cancellations, and other unforeseen circumstances.

7. Check Visa Requirements: Verify if you need a visa to enter Switzerland. Check the visa requirements based on your nationality and the duration of your stay.

8. Sports and Entertainment: Create a list of activities and hobbies you want. Zermatt offers many activities, such as skiing, hiking, and cultural exploration.

9. Dining Reservations: If you want to try a specific restaurant, especially Panorama Restaurant, please make a reservation in advance.

10. Weather Considerations: Be prepared for varying weather conditions, especially if you plan outdoor activities. Check the weather forecast closer to your travel dates.

11. Guided Tours and Activities: Research guided tours and activities available in Zermatt. Local guides can enhance your experience and provide insights into the region.

12. Language and Currency: Swiss German is the primary language, but English is widely spoken. The currency is the Swiss Franc (CHF). Familiarize yourself with basic phrases and currency exchange rates.

13. Responsible Tourism: Responsible tourism. Take care of the environment, comply with local laws, and promote sustainable development.

14. Local Events and Festivals: See local events and festivals happening during your visit. These cultural experiences can add depth to your trip.

15. Emergency Number: Save emergency contacts, including local police and medical services. Find out the nearest hospitals and emergency centers.

16. Pack accordingly: Pack seasonal clothing and accessories. These include basic items such as comfortable walking shoes, weather-appropriate clothing, and any special equipment suitable for the activities you plan to do.

17. Technology and Connectivity: Check the availability of internet and mobile services in Zermatt. Having a reliable connection is crucial for navigation and communication.

18. Check COVID-19 Guidelines: Stay informed about the latest COVID-19 guidelines and travel restrictions. Check for any specific measures in place for Zermatt.

19. Local Etiquette and Customs: Familiarize yourself with local etiquette and customs. Respect the environment, greet locals courteously, and adhere to any cultural norms.

By carefully planning your visit to Zermatt, and considering these factors, you can ensure a delightful and memorable experience in this enchanting Alpine destination. Whether you're seeking adventure, relaxation, or cultural immersion, Zermatt has something for every traveler.